POSITIVE APPROACHES TO CONFLICT AT WORK

How can we sensitively manage different types of conflict to create a more harmonious and efficient workplace?

Workplace conflict can arise when people with different backgrounds or values disagree on approaches, interests, and ideas. This can result in inefficient collaboration and may even impact workers' mental health. This book covers a range of scenarios around how conflict at work can manifest and discusses approaches to managing these in the right way to improve motivation, productivity, and the overall wellbeing of employees. It explores contemporary research, theory, and models, and includes exercises for critical reflection to aid understanding. In so doing, it encourages leaders to take responsibility for addressing different types of conflict and how to do so with sensitivity. It also signals when other approaches, such as coaching, mentoring and mediation may be necessary and, when appropriate, signposts to internal formal processes such as disciplinary and grievance procedures.

This accessible and practical book assists business owners, managers, and leaders in effectively navigating conflict management within the work environment.

Suzanna Tan is an accredited executive coach with over 15 years of in-house and freelance private and public sector work developing leaders through coaching and training. She also has 25 years of experience in the finance sector working across virtual teams, in a matrix environment, and in various business unit functions.

BUSINESS IN MIND

Supporting mental health at work is part of good management, and is essential for productivity, sustainable growth and employee wellbeing. The books in this series are at the intersection between clinical and workplace practice, and apply what we know about the benefits of supporting employee resilience and wellbeing in a diverse range of environments and roles. Titles focus on the application of research and evidence in business environments, and explore approaches that provide a practical way for individuals, managers and corporate leaders to understand the role of mental wellbeing in the workplace.

SERIES EDITOR:
Bob Thomson

BOOKS IN THE SERIES:
Positive Approaches to Conflict at Work
Suzanna Tan

POSITIVE APPROACHES TO CONFLICT AT WORK

Suzanna Tan

R Routledge
Taylor & Francis Group

LONDON AND NEW YORK

Designed cover image: Getty Images - vencavolrab

First published 2026
by Routledge
4 Park Square, Milton Park, Abingdon, Oxon OX14 4RN

and by Routledge
605 Third Avenue, New York, NY 10158

Routledge is an imprint of the Taylor & Francis Group, an informa business

© 2026 Suzanna Tan

British Library Cataloguing-in-Publication Data
A catalogue record for this book is available from the British Library

ISBN: 978-1-041-09485-2 (hbk)
ISBN: 978-1-916925-23-6 (pbk)
ISBN: 978-1-041-05646-1 (ebk)

DOI: 10.4324/9781041056461

Typeset in Joanna
by codeMantra

CONTENTS

ABOUT THE AUTHOR

Suzanna Tan has spent 25 years in the financial sector and also works as a freelance executive coach, coach tutor, and workplace mediator. Her journey into coaching began over 15 years ago when she was a line manager supporting her team. She holds a Diploma in Coaching and a Master's in Career Development and Coaching Studies from the University of Warwick. As an accredited executive coach by the Association for Coaching and a qualified workplace mediator, she enjoys helping others navigate the complexities of work, refine their authentic leadership approach, and advance their careers.

Series Editor

Bob Thomson was a Professor at Warwick Business School. He is an experienced and accredited coach, coaching supervisor, and mediator. He is the author of a number of books on coaching and management.

ACKNOWLEDGEMENTS

Writing this book has been a journey filled with moments of inspiration and countless challenges turning my thoughts into coherent words for readers.

I am immensely grateful to Bob Thomson for his unwavering patience, wisdom, and encouragement at every step, enabling me to trust in myself so I could find inspiration to develop better content. It has been an absolute privilege and a career highlight to have had the opportunity to work with him.

Thank you to everyone at Critical Publishing for believing in this project and providing the opportunity to work on this. Special thanks to Julia Morris and Lily Harrison, for their support. My gratitude also goes to everyone at Routledge for bringing this book to life with its publication. Special thanks also go to Rebecca Marsh and Grace Collier.

I am also thankful to the individuals I've had the pleasure of working with throughout my career, particularly the coachees who have placed their trust in me. Our shared experiences have been a constant source of learning and growth for me.

Most importantly, to my family and friends – thank you for taking an interest in what I do and for being a listening ear when I needed it most.

INTRODUCTION

I'm naturally uncomfortable in conflict situations, especially when I find myself at the heart of them. Early on in my corporate career, I would often shy away from conflict altogether, pretending everything was fine. If there were disagreements within the team, I'd quietly step back and stay on the sidelines, letting others take the lead in resolving or working through the disagreement. I'd often see both sides of the situation, feeling unable to take a stance.

As I gained experience, I forced myself to get involved, but I can't say I got much better at it. On one occasion, I was labelled an *overprotective mother hen*, as I attempted to face conflict head-on when challenged on a decision relating to one of my team. Another time, I had caused conflict unintentionally which resulted in the matter being blown out of context with tears all around. Most of the time I'd try to prevent any risk of disagreement in an attempt to ensure there was no need for conflict to arise. I rarely handled conflict well at work.

Later in my career, through the coaching sessions and workshops I've delivered, I came to realise and accept that conflict at work is not only common but also very normal. Listening to clients navigate their own conflict situations has shown me there is no one magic approach to apply.

Furthermore, there are numerous research articles and books on tried and tested approaches and theories on handling conflict. But when I was in the thick of it at work, I had no idea that any of these existed. What I have now learned is that there are so many positive approaches we can choose to handle conflict at work. Many of these will be positive approaches that anyone can adopt and incorporate into their daily working lives. While I may have struggled with handling my own conflicts back when I was working in the corporate world, I've found that I am far better at supporting others to deal with their own conflict situations since I've become a coach.

The idea for writing this book was to provide working people with some practical, straightforward approaches to consider and use when dealing with conflict at work. My hope is that the strategies and insights introduced in this book will help you navigate the conflict you encounter at work. To help illustrate some of these approaches, I've included some case studies which have been drawn from common scenarios I've encountered in my own work, my work with clients, stories from friends and colleagues, and situations I've researched. Although the names and all details have been changed to protect privacy, you might find some situations strikingly familiar. If you spot any relevance in any of the examples, this might be because the types of conflict I describe are universal. They happen in workplaces everywhere, and you may even recognise aspects of your own personal experiences in them.

When using this book, it would be useful to read Part 1 first, and then the rest of the book as a reference guide which you can dip in and out of when and as required. The three parts are:

- Part 1 covers some background on conflict and useful tools to consider.
- Part 2 explores how you can manage conflict within yourself, with another person, with others and then at an organisational level.
- Part 3 introduces some third-party approaches to consider such as coaching, mentoring, sponsors, mediation and other measures.

I wish you all the best in navigating your conflict situations at work, and hope that you'll find some of the positive approaches in this book useful to you.

PART 1

1

CONFLICT IS NORMAL

Introduction

Conflict is inevitable. Why, how, and when conflict occurs can be simple or extremely complex, straightforward or multi-dimensional. To manage conflict effectively, it's useful to recognise and appreciate the differentiating factors and layers of complexity that underlie what is happening in any given situation.

The word conflict stems from the Latin words:

- *con* bringing together
- *confligere* to strike together
- *conflictus* clash

Simply put, conflict is any form of disagreement, no matter how large or small it is. Conflict often produces friction due to differing opinions or incompatibility, which can negatively impact mental health and well-being. However conflict managed the right way and with sensitivity,

DOI: 10.4324/9781041056461-2

when required, can have a positive result on problem-solving and innovation through increased understanding of each other. Positive impacts on mental health and wellbeing can be experienced through personal growth and learning in resolving or working through disagreement, strengthened relationships where further trust is built, and increased self-awareness and support to build resilience. This book focuses on exploring how to manage conflict in the workplace.

Poorly managed conflict in the workplace

Part 2 of this book covers how people experience conflict at work within themselves, with other people, or with the organisation. When conflict is not managed well, people can start reassessing their priorities, and when they are no longer satisfied with ignoring disparities of what they want from their work versus what they actually feel about their work, they may leave their organisations resulting in the loss of talented staff. Disillusioned workers in the UK have been striking over issues such as pay across sectors including the railways, teaching, and healthcare since 2022. The impact on the mental health and wellbeing of those involved and those affected by these strikes is far-reaching. Thus, conflict at work not only impacts those in the workplace, but people who are reliant on their services.

The expedited shift to hybrid working since the COVID-19 pandemic has affected how conflict is managed at work. It could be expected that being in different locations and being together less of the time, results in less conflict because people work more remotely and in silos. However, the unintended consequences of this way of working can result in disagreements left unattended and not handled in a timely way, or disparities being unnoticed or ignored until it feels too late to manage them effectively.

Cost of conflict in the workplace

Recent studies have been able to estimate and quantify the repercussions of conflict in the workplace. There is a report from Acas that illustrates this well called, 'Estimating the costs of workplace conflict' (Saundry and Urwin, 2021), which is based on research, and the Chartered Institute of Personnel and Development's (CIPD) early 2020 publication 'Managing conflict in the modern workplace' (CIPD, 2020). Saundry and Urwin estimated workplace conflict costs UK employers £28.5 billion each year. This averages at an annual cost of £1,000 per employee. They also estimated:

- About 10 million people had experienced workplace conflict, with around half of them experiencing stress, anxiety, or depression.
- As a result of conflict, almost 486,000 people resign annually costing organisations approximately £2.6 billion to replace them.
- The lost output and time to upskill new employees costs a further £12.2 billion.
- 874,000 employees are off sick each year costing organisations £2.2 billion.
- There is also additional cost estimated of between £590 million and £2.3 billion per year of reduced productivity from those remaining at work but are impacted with stress, anxiety, or depression as a result of conflict in the workplace.

The commercial numbers are stark. But what is even more sobering are the ramifications on employees.

Consequences of workplace conflict on mental health and wellbeing

When people experience conflict at work, it can affect their mental health and wellbeing. The level of this will depend on how that person perceives and handles conflict. It will also be dependent on their level of skills and the strategies they have to support them to manage conflict. Prior experiences from being in conflict situations and whether these have been positive or negative outcomes for them can also affect how they manage conflict. This can manifest in how people behave and think, and you may have seen this in yourself or those you work with during or after conflict situations.

In situations of conflict, individuals may experience stress or anxiety due to a sense of pressure or perceived threat, leading to feelings of concern or mental strain. Feelings of stress or anxiety can be mild or more severe and even result in physical symptoms such as headaches, stomach tension, breathing difficulties, or the inability to rest or sleep. This can lead to depression for those who cannot handle conflict effectively for themselves or are frequently in conflict situations. Feelings such as lack of interest, sadness, helplessness, or tiredness can be experienced, which can result in poorer performance at or absence from work and can even spill into and negatively impinge on their home life.

Some people can experience reduced self-esteem and resort to working in isolation to purposely avoid conflict situations. Those who are unable to handle conflict effectively may take disagreements personally or even as criticisms of how they operate at work. This can have repercussions on their self-worth and result in them withdrawing from situations of conflict or other work activity as their confidence erodes. With less communication with others, the isolation from the continuous lack of interaction with colleagues may produce a downwards spiral. To stop the spiral there needs to be a break in the pattern or changes in the way people work, with deliberate steps or interventions to regain control.

While conflict at work can affect mental health and wellbeing, the extent and impact can be managed by how conflict is handled. By addressing conflict in a healthy and optimal way, with strategies to get the best out of the situation, you can minimise its effects and even create some benefits.

Conflict is all around us

It is worth considering how the presence of conflict has always been a part of our world, i.e. it is normal. Plants in forests compete for the daylight they require for photosynthesis to survive, with those growing the tallest thriving and overshadowing those beneath. They also compete for water and nutrients in the ground and their proximity to other plants can be determined through their root systems. Those that need different nutrients may have intertwined roots, while those that compete for the same nutrients move away from each other. With animals, the natural competition to procreate is an instinctive drive that ensures future generations survive. The strongest and fittest genes win. Natural selection has ensured the organisms that adapt to their environment are more likely to thrive and survive throughout generations. An interesting Netflix four-part documentary called Chimp Empire (2023) follows how chimpanzees across a forest in Uganda navigate the complexities of family and social politics while competing for the same resources. Although it can be argued that it is based on somewhat primal instincts and behaviours, some of the ways in which they handle conflict can be related to our modern way of life.

Why conflict occurs

Conflict is often perceived negatively which can influence how it is dealt with. Our negative connotations of conflict could stem from our primitive and evolutionary responses. When disagreements occur, the reptilian part of the brain produces a fight, flight or freeze response. Some thrive on the conflict, some avoid it at all costs, and others are debilitated by it. This is explained well in *The Chimp Paradox* where Steve Peters (2013) illustrates how the brain has three different entities which are the Human, the Chimp, and the Computer:

1. The Human part (pre-frontal cortex of the brain) is where logical and rational thinking occurs.
2. The Chimp part (limbic area of the brain) is where the emotional, reactive and impulsive reactions occur such as fear, frustration and anger, and can often be irrational.
3. The Computer part (parietal part of the brain) stores memories and beliefs that influence how we think and behave and this can sometimes occur unconsciously.

In conflict situations, the Chimp can cause the initial reaction to what is happening as emotions overwhelm how people feel. Managing the Chimp and engaging the Human to think more rationally can help to calm and manage the situation. The Computer is useful as past experiences can help people think through what's worked well previously, or consider using alternative approaches to handling a situation.

Conflict is innate in our lives. Accepting this can be the first step to appreciating its intricacies and how to handle them. Conflict needs careful management, and conflict in the workplace must be handled with even more sensitivity because there are many additional factors at stake including a multitude of different influences that drive how people feel, think, and behave.

How our backgrounds determine our natural approach to conflict

Conflict in social settings arises because, more often than not, our communities have grown and developed to include a mix of people with different backgrounds, values, interests, motivations, perceptions, and ideas. When interacting with each other, there will be occasions when people disagree. People are social beings connected to each other through relationships, regardless of whether they want this or like it. From birth, people learn to manage relationships in order to survive.

Family

Within any family which has a shared background each member of the family is quite different. There is a pecking order in a family, which is not always determined by birth order, intelligence, or natural ability. People will have been involved in different types of relationships with parents, siblings, grandparents, and other extended family. Although values can be derived from family, they can also differ due to individual personalities and interests. Differences and disagreements occur early on in life, and thus people are naturally exposed to conflict resulting from different values, interests, motivations, perceptions, and ideas. For example, parent and child conflict could have occurred throughout childhood which might include disagreements on educational or career choices, or perhaps choice of friends. If you have brothers or sisters, you'll be familiar with sibling rivalry where disputes over perceived favouritism from parents or competition for resources such as food or treats occur. Often, the power dynamic of parents or the pecking order or age compared to siblings can determine the outcome of any disagreement. There is less likelihood that someone will go against a parent who threatens and has the power to take privileges away. Or perhaps you are more likely to give in to a much younger sibling who you deem may not understand the situation.

These experiences repeated throughout childhood can influence patterns of thinking and behaviour. Conflict management begins early on and through these experiences individuals develop the skills to handle conflict – such as communication skills through listening and negotiating with parents or siblings, empathy and emotional regulation to deal with different people, problem-solving to resolve issues, and resilience and adaptability to get through the outcomes. However, the level of effectiveness of these skills will differ and influence how you develop your conflict management approach. For example, some people develop unhelpful attitudes and behaviours to avoid conflict by quickly compromising or removing themselves from situations. Others may develop more forceful tactics such as dominating or aggressive behaviour to control conflict situations. Some people become pacifiers who learn to calm situations. In families, particularly when there are siblings, you may notice how family members handle conflict differently. Only children do not have the chance to develop sibling relationships, which can have both advantages and drawbacks. On the positive side, their viewpoints may not face challenges which can lead to increased confidence, but on the negative side they may have fewer opportunities to cultivate diverse perspectives and conflict resolution skills.

Friends outside of work

Then, consider adding another dimension by including the friends you've encountered throughout your life's journey. This introduces a further array of disagreements and varying viewpoints to navigate. Friends come from different backgrounds with different cultures and upbringings. Different interests become more apparent as people develop, for example, different tastes in food, types of television shows, music and hobbies. With friends, compromise depends on the stake you have in your relationship or the value you put on it. With established friendships there may be a higher level of importance put on maintaining relationships, and the ability to truly be who you are with them can also help when negotiating your way.

Workplace

The next layer to consider is the workplace environment. Here, relationships with colleagues are just one aspect. Added to this are the pressures of resource limitations, urgent tasks, and sometimes incompatible objectives, making conflict more likely. Work environments can draw out different facets of people's personalities. Authenticity can be tested because the demands of professionalism at work may lead you to behave in ways that differ from your behaviour outside of the workplace. How often have you thought that you would not have accepted something in your personal life, but accept it at work? Or that you would manage a situation differently if it was not work? The complexities and added importance of the factors at work play heavily into how situations are managed. People have different drivers and reasons for being at work. For some it could just be a way of making income, for others it could be about developing a career or making a difference. Whatever the reason or reasons, these factors influence how conflict can arise and how it is managed.

Furthermore, the relationship dynamics with colleagues play a key part in how conflict is managed. For example, how you deal with colleagues may be different from how you deal with your line manager or direct reports. Whether you are the manager or direct report, or sometimes both, communication approaches, expectations of what's required and differing opinions on things such as decision-making, workload, recognition, and autonomy, can create conflict between people.

The importance of stakeholder relationships at work

Building good relationships at work is a fundamental way in which you can get things done. Not only are they important for work, but having good stakeholder relationships is good for mental health and wellbeing. But how close and social should relationships be at work? Whether friendships or non-social colleague relationships are formed, there can be merit in all forms of cooperative stakeholder relationships.

Work friends

Gallup research, 'The increasing importance of a best friend at work' (Patel and Plowman, 2022), indicated that having a best friend at work is strongly linked to business outcomes, including profitability, safety, inventory control, and retention.

> Employees who have a best friend at work are significantly more likely to:
>
> - engage customers and internal partners
> - get more done in less time
> - support a safe workplace with fewer accidents and reliability concerns
> - innovate and share ideas
> - have fun while at work
>
> (Patel and Plowman, 2022)

Having friends at work is a controversial topic with which you may or may not agree. My belief is that you do not have to go as far as cultivating a best friend at work, but friends at work can be very positive for mental health and wellbeing. Often more contact time is spent at work with colleagues than at home with family or with friends outside of work. The friends we make at work may not last after you or they leave the workplace, but people you connect with on a social level at work can make the time you spend there more enjoyable. Work friendships can be deepened with social activities outside of work, however, this is not always necessary as there are opportunities to connect and bond in everyday working life.

By developing friends at work you can cultivate trust and a sense of belonging as you support each other through difficult times. In conflict situations, they can be a great source of support. Tom Rath's research in his book, *Vital Friends* (Rath, 2006), describes the different types of friends you can have at work to support you for better outcomes. Here are some of the different types that may come in handy.

- *Builders* to motivate, support your development, and are interested in your success.
- *Champions* who will sponsor and help others see how good you are.
- *Collaborators* with similar interests to you will support and work with you.
- *Connectors* to help extend your network and help build bridges to get what you want.
- *Energizers* to provide energy that can optimise your outputs and help boost you up when times are hard.
- *Mind Openers* who stretch your viewpoints, open up opportunities that challenge your thinking and outlook.
- *Navigators* who provide advice and direction, like mentors.

Conversely, there can be occasions when work friends can be detrimental, especially when it comes to how conflict is managed. Friendships can sometimes determine how open and honest you are as you may not want to upset each other, which can lead to adverse effects on business outcomes. Maintaining clear boundaries with expectations of how to handle disagreements can help foster psychological safety to explore and get to the outcomes required. When dealing with conflict at work, it can be helpful to agree together that a more professional approach should be taken so that the familiarity of friendships does not impede on work obligations.

Furthermore, when an inner circle of friends at work forms, this can be both powerful and dangerous at the same time. Those within the circle can be seen as cliquey and impenetrable or favoured through having greater autonomy, freedom, and trust. Those outside the circle can feel left out and excluded from important decisions. Group think or collusion can occur as like-minded people are drawn together by their thoughts, feelings and goals within the inner circle. That common perspective, or the way you always do things, can also result in limited innovation.

Acquaintances at work

Acquaintances formed at work are just as important when it comes to disagreements that may arise. Work acquaintances are people you know of and who know of you. They can be limited to specific contexts such as another stakeholder on a project you've been on, or a fellow line manager who you see at annual year-end performance reviews. These colleagues who you know on a more casual basis are important to maintain, as this network will help when dealing with conflict. Some people prefer to maintain only acquaintances at work to keep work purely professional. You will be aware of what each other can do, and what they are good at or who they know or work with. When engaged in disagreement with acquaintances, the additional pressure of friendship does not get in the way, and managing the conflict can be less complex as it is less personal. Acquaintances can provide a more neutral and objective perspective which has no emotional ties or biases. They can also provide more diverse insights and ideas as they may be from other teams or departments, which can lead to innovative solutions to conflict situations.

Stakeholder management

Some people naturally build and maintain good stakeholder relationships at work, for example, the director who can casually engage in conversation with one of the team, without making them feel scared or on edge, or a colleague who seems to know everybody and how to influence or pave the way when there is a difficult issue with a team or on a project. For those who are not naturally able to do this, there are many tools to help with developing stakeholder relationships.

Immediate Team
- Line Manager
- Team Peer 1
- Team Peer 2
- Direct Report 1
- Direct Report 2
- Direct Report 3

Learning and Development
- Coach
- Mentor
- Human Resources Business Partner

You

Project A

	Project Manager	Commercial Lead
Accountable Executive	Compliance Lead	Operations Lead
Business Analyst	Legal Lead	Customer Lead
Sales Lead	Public Relations Lead	Communications Lead

Project B

Accountable Executive	Project Manager

External Stakeholders

	Regulatory Contact 1
Press 1	Regulatory Contact 2
Press 2	Agency 1
Consumer Action Group Lead	Agency 2

Customer/Client
- Frontline Sales Lead
- Customer Segment 1
- Customer Segment 2

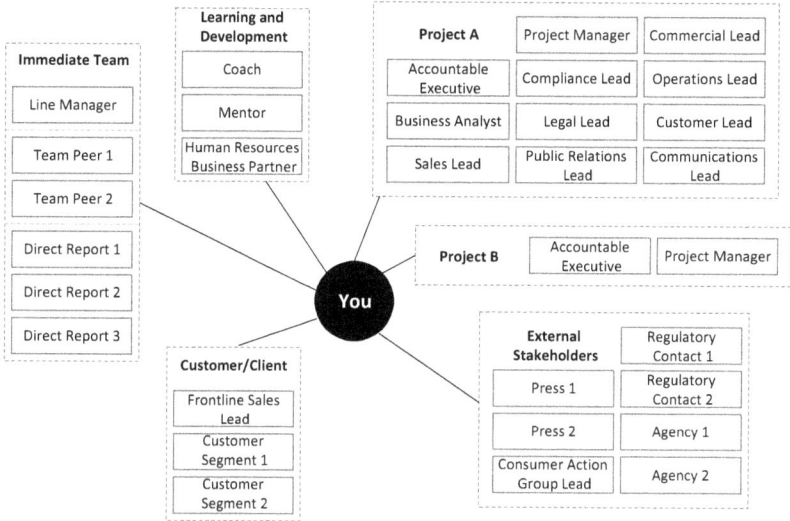

Figure 1.1 Example of a stakeholder map

A stakeholder map of everyone you need to interact with in your role can be used as a living tool for managing different relationships. It can consist of stakeholders such as your line manager, peers in your team, other people in other teams across functions or business units, people outside your organisation, such as suppliers or regulators, and even customers or clients. Your approach to this can be in whatever format works for you. The example provided in Figure 1.1 is a simple map which can help when you start thinking of the groups of people in your stakeholder map. Yours may be more or less complex than the example provided for illustration purposes here.

In times of conflict, stakeholders are key to helping you understand how to manage the conflict or to support you in managing the conflict with sensitivity. The next chapter will build on how to organise stakeholders to help develop and build relationships with them, which will be useful when it comes to managing conflict at work.

Country and cultural dynamics

In the virtual and multi-cultural workplace, cultural differences influence how we work and conflicts can arise without anyone realising why. This is sometimes termed cross-cultural or intercultural conflict. Due to different values and beliefs driving how people think, feel and behave, there can be a lack of awareness, unconscious bias or unwillingness to understand. People tend to view or interpret other people's values, behaviours and beliefs through their own cultural lens. Ethnocentrism stems from someone believing that only their way of doing something is right or that their culture dictates the only right way of thinking, feeling and behaving. At a micro level, people have different expectations of each other due to conflicting cultural beliefs. This can escalate with differing political and religious beliefs, and on a macro level, this type of conflict at its worst can result in war. The complexities of cultural differences are often unconscious. It is also highly contextual and depends on the particular situations you are found in and the outcomes that are required. It is important not to generalise or stereotype when working across cultures. People may have underlying cultural ways of doing things, but may have adapted their approach when working with people from different cultures.

Healthy workplace conflict

Workplace conflict, when handled well, is necessary to create better outcomes. By considering diverse perspectives, creative thinking, and thorough evaluation of the situation can occur. It reduces the risk of group think, which is when people accept and go with the consensus without challenging or thinking things through from different angles. It can also produce continuous improvement through better communication between stakeholders collaborating to get to better solutions, thus, creating a healthier environment that can positively support mental health and wellbeing.

Getting to a point where conflict is healthy is the key aim of this book. The Healthy Conflict Triangle is a simple reminder of how to evaluate what is happening when a conflict arises at work. Reflecting on what type of conflict it is in terms of the influence it has on the relationships of those involved can be the starting point for how to manage the situation.

- *Unresolved* conflict is where conflict is not dealt with and can result in issues not worked through or ignored with unsatisfactory outcomes. This might happen when someone avoids or accommodates the other. When conflict is unresolved the situation may linger and even escalate if not dealt with appropriately.

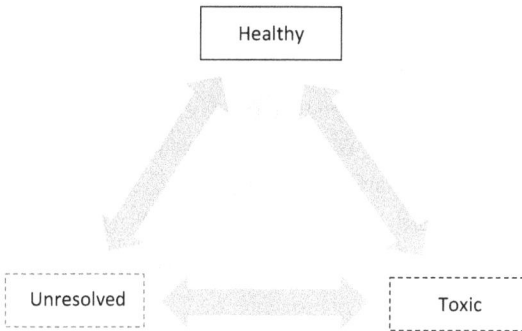

Figure 1.2 Healthy Conflict Triangle

- *Toxic* conflict is where the situation is unsatisfactory for one or both parties; it is extremely unhealthy for everyone involved and may significantly affect their mental health and wellbeing. Sometimes it has become toxic because the relationship has broken down too far, or when one person is competing and exhibiting undesirable behaviours.
- *Healthy* conflict is where those involved are able to have constructive debate or dialogue on how to move forward to resolve the conflict. There needs to be psychological safety so everyone can freely express their ideas and opinions, and trust that everyone wants to do what is best in terms of the issue at hand.

Healthy conflict is considered the most effective for working through disagreements at work as the collaborative and respectful approach enables people to work together on outcomes. It may be that the conflict moves to being unresolved or toxic depending on how much trust and respect there is between the disagreeing parties. As we move through the chapters, this approach is used to consider how to move to a place of healthy conflict, where conflict management strategies and outcomes can have a more positive effect on mental health, wellbeing and business outcomes.

Summary

Whether we are comfortable or not so comfortable with conflict, it is something that will always occur in the workplace. Therefore, through understanding how and why disagreement occurs, you can start to manage or resolve it using positive approaches.

Key takeaways

- Conflict is inevitable in the workplace.
- Not only is there a mental health and wellbeing cost of poorly handled workplace conflict, there is also commercial cost due to lower productivity and stifled innovation.
- Conflict is influenced by how people think, feel, and behave which stems from backgrounds and relationships with family, friends, work friends, and cultures.
- People handle conflict differently and there are a number of internal and external factors that influence what can be done to handle it with sensitivity.

Reflective exercise

1. Think of an example of when you have been involved in conflict in the workplace.
2. Why do you think it occurred?
3. How did you manage it?
4. What impact do you think it had on your and the other person's or people's mental health and wellbeing?
5. What key takeaways or learnings did you acquire from the experience?

References

Saundry, R, and Urwin, P (11 May 2021). Estimating the costs of workplace conflict. Report for Acas. Centre for Employment Research, University of Westminster. Available at: https://www.acas.org.uk/page-download/850?1689609331602 (accessed 25 September 2023).

Chimp Empire (2023). Netflix. Available at: https://www.netflix.com/gb/title/81311783 (accessed 25 September 2023).

CIPD (2020). Managing conflict in the modern workplace. Available at: https://www. cipd.org/uk/knowledge/reports/managing-workplace-conflict-report/ (accessed 25 September 2023).

Patel, A, and Plowman, S (17 August 2022). The increasing importance of a best friend at work. Report by GALLUP. Available at: https://www.gallup.com/workplace/397058/increasing-importance-best-friend-work.aspx (accessed 25 September 2023).

Peters, S (2013). The Chimp Paradox: The Mind Management Program to Help You Achieve Success, Confidence, and Happiness. Jeremy P Tarcher/Penguin.

Rath, T (2006). Vital Friends – The People You Can't Afford to Live Without. Gallup Press.

2

USEFUL TOOLS

Introduction

Many theories and models have been developed by philosophers and sociologists studying conflict in society and at work. This chapter begins with different ways of viewing conflict by identifying which stage the conflict is at and categorising the type of conflict being experienced. Next, a popular tool for handling conflict is introduced bringing a choice of five different approaches to use. Finally, the chapter concludes with how to understand and manage stakeholder relationships, which is critical to understand as a foundation for dealing with conflict. These ideas will be built on throughout the book while exploring different conflict situations and positive approaches to handling them.

Within my coaching practice, clients frequently present scenarios of conflict encountered at work. They can find themselves grappling with discomfort stemming from disagreements, and struggling to navigate, resolve or progress them. Typically, their primary objective is to alleviate their uneasiness while safeguarding their interests. Some may have already

DOI: 10.4324/9781041056461-3

started to notice adverse effects on their mental health and well-being. De Dreu et al. (2004) discussed this in the *International Journal of Conflict Management*, highlighting studies exploring the relationship between conflict and an individual's wellbeing, together with the consequences of ignoring this over time (De Drue et al., 2004). What may begin as psychosomatic complaints, such as negative feelings and body reactions like quickened heart rates, headaches, or sweating, can escalate to more serious feelings of burnout like anxiety or gastrointestinal symptoms. A more recent study by Kerman et al. (2022) for the *International Journal of Environmental Research and Public Health*, highlighted conflict experienced at work can impair sleep which is critical to maintaining good health and wellbeing.

Moreover, when mental health and wellbeing is negatively impacted, that in itself can be a contributing factor to conflict. When run down and tired, there is a risk that behaviour is compromised, leading to unintended outcomes. Recognising these initial feelings can provide a starting point to address situations proactively, rather than allowing them to escalate to a toxic state of conflict as outlined in the Healthy Conflict Triangle in Chapter 1. In the heat of conflict, there is a risk that rational reasoning gets lost. The tools introduced here offer practical and positive approaches to managing conflict at work in a healthy way, conducive to overall mental health and wellbeing. Often, the experience of being in a conflict situation suddenly arises and there is a risk of the tendency to dive into resolving it without realising the best approach to take. Thus, it can be helpful to reflect on and be aware of these four considerations:

1. Stage – the point at which the conflict has developed to or is at.
2. Type – categorising what the conflict is specifically about.
3. Preference – preferred approaches to use to handle the conflict.
4. Power – understanding the stakeholders involved and their level of influence on the conflict.

Stage of conflict

The first step is to identify the stage at which the conflict is at before uncovering what is genuinely happening for all those involved. There are two ideas I find useful to use depending on the conflict situation. The first is a basic categorisation of *pre-*, *during-*, and *post-conflict* stages.

- Pre-conflict happens before disagreement starts to surface, although there may be some tell-tale signs of this by individuals keeping quiet and not voicing opinions, delays in timelines as those involved find their way, or feelings of uncertainty or unease.
- During-conflict occurs when disagreement is evident, as people try to work through or challenge each other to find a way through.
- Post-conflict is when the disagreement is over, whether it has been resolved or not. If unresolved, there is the chance of it going back to the during-conflict stage again.

An alternative concept is provided by Louis Pondy (1967), who explains conflict as a dynamic process with five stages: *latent, perceived, felt, manifest, and aftermath.*

1. Latent is when the conflict has not emerged, and there is potential for it to evolve due to underlying factors such as limited resources, autonomy, power or control desires, or diverging objectives from those involved.
2. Perceived is where there is a cognitive shift as the conflict progresses and those involved become aware of it. This happens in two ways: (i) conflict without latent conditions where misunderstanding or differing perceptions of the situation arise between those involved; or (ii) conflict resulting from latent factors, where those involved are not aware of it yet, which can be a risk to the project, team or organisation.
3. Felt occurs as those involved experience it emotionally in different ways such as anger, tension, stress or frustration. Often, cooperation reduces and relatively minor conflicts can start to grow into bigger ones.
4. Manifest results in more tangible forms as it moves beyond emotions, adopting forms such as verbal aggression or tactics which obstruct the other's objectives or frustrate them.
5. Aftermath brings repercussions of what has happened as a result of the conflict. There could be long-term damage or if resolution has been good for everyone, basis for future cooperation and better relationships.

Figure 2.1 depicts both approaches and conflict grows from left to right. As conflict evolves, those involved may not be aware conflict is developing in the pre or latent stages. This is key to note because there may be times when

PRE		DURING		POST
Stage 1	Stage 2	Stage 3	Stage 4	Stage 5
LATENT	PERCEIVED	FELT	MANIFEST	AFTERMATH

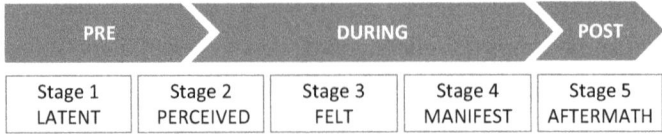

Figure 2.1 Adapted from the five conflict stages article by Pondy LR, 'Organizational conflict: Concepts and models' (1967)

you or others may not appreciate there is an issue at hand. The time involved during each stage is variable, and it is not necessary to go through each one. When working with clients they find it valuable to categorise or break down situations and how they have occurred. Raising awareness of how they and others are feeling or behaving, can lay the foundations for constructive positive approaches to help handle conflict situations. Clients often come with a scenario where the conflict is at the during or manifest stage, and those involved have already resorted to undesirable actions as their chimp has jumped into action and rational thinking from their human brain has not kicked in, as touched on in Chapter 1. It can be useful to go back to previous stages to explore how situations escalate. Gaining greater awareness of how those involved experienced the initial stages will aid in rationally choosing the best approach to use and may prevent the conflict from escalating.

When choosing a way of identifying the conflict's stage, you may have your own approaches. My preference is to start by using pre-, during-, and post-conflict, as it is relatively simpler and quicker for clients to apply and remember. However, when deeper exploration is required I switch to Pondy's five stages because reflecting on these can add more depth to what is happening.

CASE STUDY A

Cassie and Terry identify the stage of conflict

Cassie and Terry were peers who worked in the same team for three years and got along well, even considering each other as friends. Their line manager resigned and the opportunity to apply for a promotion arose. Both applied, which set the scenario for pre or latent stage of the impending conflict. Although both were supportive of each other applying, underlying factors were already there, such as of lack of resources, as there was only one position. Cassie was offered the position and although Terry magnanimously congratulated her, both knew difficulties lay ahead, the pre or perceived stage. Very soon, the during or felt stage was underway as Cassie tried to make her stance in her new position of authority. It was at this point that she started to feel anxious about how to manage situations with Terry.

Here, we find two colleagues who have been peers and one gets promoted becoming the other's line manager. It may begin as pre or latent conflict and as they become accustomed to working with each other in the new dynamic, but it can quickly escalate through the during or perceived and felt stages. Identifying where in the conflict lifecycle the situation stands or through reflecting on what happened at each stage, provides increased levels of awareness together with valuable insight of how the conflict develops. For Cassie, she was able to use this analysis to talk through the situation with Terry to gain his perspective about what was happening.

Type of conflict

In conflict situations, the underlying issues are often obscured by what is going on. Have you ever been in the midst of trying to resolve a conflict with someone, but cannot make headway as both of you seem to be getting further apart from resolution? While disagreements can be complex and do not always fit into an easily identifiable box, attempting to categorise them allows you to strategise more effective approaches. In a *Harvard Business Review* guide, Amy Gallo (2017) categorised conflict into that of *relationship, task, process* and *status*.

- Relationship conflict is interpersonal or emotional in nature, where negative feelings become involved resulting from negative behaviour. When working with others, they will most likely also want their own way and come from a place which they believe is right. It's useful to think of their perspective and instead of 'treat others the way *you* want to be treated', flip it to 'treat others the way *they* want to be treated'.
- Task conflict is most common at work and Gallo explains these as disagreements over agendas, success measures or prioritisation, and there may be differing opinions on what these may be.
- Process conflict relates to how something is done, such as managing a project, implementing a policy or running a meeting. She highlights

that process can be confused with task, 'You think you're arguing over the outcome when really you can't agree on how to make the decision' (Gallo, 2017).

- Status conflict is about perceived or power dynamics causing disagreement due to roles, level of authority, influence or recognition expected. These clashes often occur at work, especially in competitive cultures or where authority lines are unclear.

Recognising and categorising conflict using these four types can support how to approach the situation. However, what if the lines about what the conflict is about are not clear-cut, for example, if one party thinks it's a status conflict and the other thinks it's relationship? Let's go back to the Cassie and Terry case study to explore this.

CASE STUDY A (CONTINUED)

Cassie and Terry identify the type of conflict

With her change in authority, Cassie struggled when it came to working with Terry. She was fine with her other direct reports as they were not friends and she maintained a purely professional approach working with them. One example was when she reassigned her work across the team while she backfilled her previous position. She found Terry pushed back too readily suggesting others were given responsibilities he did not want. He was direct and forthright about it and Cassie struggled to influence him to do otherwise, even when she used rational facts such as his skill set and ability to take on specific tasks better than others. She was frustrated and began to question their friendship and her capabilities of being an effective line manager to him.

It started to impact her mental health and wellbeing, which is when she initiated coaching. She thought perhaps Terry was taking advantage of their friendship, to pick and choose his additional responsibilities and it could be a relationship conflict. Or it could be due to her new hierarchical position causing her to take a different approach when speaking to Terry resulting in a status conflict? Her approach was to have an honest conversation with Terry, and it turned out it was a process issue from his perspective. He disagreed with how Cassie reassigned the tasks on her own without consulting the team. This was a revelation to her as she had not considered that or the impact of her actions.

What can initially feel like one conflict type, can be perceived differently by another. Gallo's categories can be useful to reflect on. I also find aligning to the principles or values of where clients work can be relatable as there is consistency in language. For example, if an organisation has values of excellence, efficiency, collaboration, and fairness, and they are applied to Cassie and Terry's example, perhaps Cassie thought fairness was the issue as she believed Terry took advantage of their friendship to push back. However, the type of conflict was due to a lack of a collaborative approach in how Cassie reassigned the work. Appreciating what the conflict is about and using a form of categorisation results in a deeper understanding of what is going on, laying the foundations for how it can be approached.

Preferred approach to conflict

When dealing with conflict, individuals exhibit varying approaches. Some dislike any form of disagreement, shying away from conflict situations, others embrace it as a challenge, and some thrive on it. One of my clients worked with someone who would declare 'Let's get ready for a good fight!' which signalled an impending toxic conflict situation. However, open dialogue conducted in an environment of psychological safety, is sometimes all that's needed to have healthy conflict. A full-on debate and winning is not always necessary for a positive outcome.

One valuable tool I frequently refer to is the Thomas–Kilmann Conflict Mode Instrument (TKI model) developed by Kenneth Thomas and Ralph

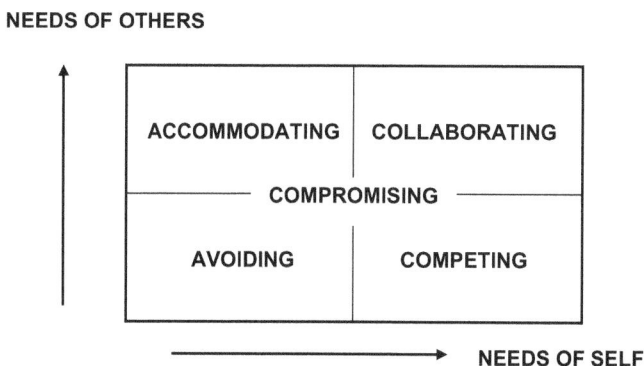

NEEDS OF OTHERS

ACCOMMODATING	COLLABORATING
COMPROMISING	
AVOIDING	COMPETING

NEEDS OF SELF

Figure 2.2 Adapted from the five ways of handling conflict, based on the Thomas–Kilmann Conflict Mode Instrument

Kilmann (1974). The TKI model provides a method to reveal preferred conflict management styles. TKI examines two distinct dimensions of assertiveness and cooperativeness, resulting in five modes of handling conflict: *avoiding, accommodating, compromising, competing,* and *collaborating.* The level of assertiveness is how much you satisfy your own needs, and the level of cooperativeness is how much you try to satisfy other's needs.

Avoiding (you lose, they lose)

In avoiding conflict mode, you tend to ignore and not deal with it at that moment. It can be chosen in situations which are more trivial or less important, when you have no power to change it, or when others may be better placed to resolve it. Avoiding can be used to park something if tensions run high, composure needs to be regained, or if time is needed to work through how to approach the disagreement. However, repeatedly avoiding dealing with disagreements can produce a negative impact on wellbeing due to constantly suppressing concerns or feelings. It can also have negative consequences on work outcomes as issues are not addressed in a timely manner or become unresolved.

Accommodating (you lose, they win)

By giving in to others or allowing them to have their way, you can maintain the relationship or increase goodwill through the accommodating conflict mode. This can be used to end conflict quickly, cut your losses, help someone else out or support them with something more important to them than to you. If this approach is often used, there can be a toll on wellbeing as the impact of giving in to others all the time from neglecting personal needs can lead to resentment. It can also contribute to an imbalance in the relationship with unproductive behaviour in the other person. Accommodating can also hinder professional growth, and stifle the ability to be innovative.

Compromising (you both lose and win)

Here, both give and take, splitting the difference with a combination of wins and losses. It can be a faster way of settling conflict efficiently;

helping maintain relationships and ensuring outcomes are fair with a balanced solution. Although on the face of it, it may seem that this is the best approach to take, it really does depend on the situation at hand. There are cons to compromising as both sides are partially satisfied, and there could be missed opportunities to be more creative by using a quick-fix approach. Consistently compromising can result in a loss of autonomy or individuality through sacrificing some of what is important.

Competing (you win, they lose)

Competing is satisfying all your needs. This is often useful in emergencies or when conflict arises due to decisions outside of your control. However, it is most used when a resolution is of most importance to you, for a believed favourable outcome and maintaining your standards or principles. Using this assertive approach may risk your relationship with the other, by losing trust or undermining other's opinions. Often a limited perspective through not considering other perspectives can result in poorer business decisions. Always competing can be draining and stressful, and the lack of adaptability to move to other approaches can result in toxic conflict situations.

Collaborating (you win, they win)

Unsurprisingly, this approach can result in good outcomes for everyone, working together to find benefits for all and enhancing relationships through the Collaborating conflict mode. It improves mutual understanding and can drive innovation and even better outcomes than originally imagined. However, it can be time-consuming as both parties must be open and flexible in their approach; and challenging to reach a consensus causing frustration when a satisfactory resolution is not achieved.

Preferred modes can be influenced by personality traits, environment, values, or cultural backgrounds. The level of satisfaction derived will depend on the situation. By reflecting on each mode, you can assess how satisfied you are in various conflict situations. It's beneficial to start by understanding your own preference before considering others. All five conflict modes are valuable, and being adaptable to move between them is a useful approach. You may begin in competing mode wanting to win and later find that if time is limited you move to compromising mode to quicken the pace. To delve deeper, www.kilmanndiagnostics.com offers extensive resources, courses, and assessments for understanding and navigating conflict in various contexts. In later chapters, we explore common example case studies to build on the advantages and drawbacks of each mode.

Stakeholder power in conflict

Have you ever wondered why certain individuals appear to have more influence or authority than others? Those higher in the hierarchy, who bear responsibilities directly correlated to their decision-making power, will naturally be in this position. But what about your peers or even those beneath you in the hierarchy? How is it that they can confidently exert their influence on various situations?

CASE STUDY B

Steve and Kwame, power dynamics in conflict

Steve had a more junior colleague in the digital team, Kwame, who was often late implementing his webpage change requests. This annoyed Steve to no end because the consequences of late changes impacted customers who were viewing incorrect information, and other colleagues who dealt with customer complaints, as well as having compliance repercussions. Furthermore, other people didn't seem to have the same issue with Kwame's work.

He avoided this conflict for many months until it came to the point where he knew he had to address it and brought the topic to coaching. Through his exploration of the situation, he realised Kwame prioritised changes from others with better relationships with him. They often called him to check his workload and updated him on their required timelines well in advance, as well as providing regular weekly updates. Kwame's preferred way of working was to have overall timelines and regular detailed updates as this enabled him to manage his workload, and most importantly, he had the power to prioritise the work. Steve realised he sent his changes on an *ad hoc* basis, presuming it would be done within the five working day service level agreement. He had not developed their relationship or provided Kwame with what he needed.

Power dynamics is at the core of most conflict theory. Examining levels of power or the perceived levels of power of individuals, or between different teams or groups, is an important factor to consider and can be pivotal in how conflict can be approached. Stakeholders are individuals with an interest in you or your project, or those who may be directly or indirectly impacted by the outcomes of a conflict situation. Knowing your stakeholders entails understanding their interests, concerns and needs. A practical tool to help manage stakeholder relationships is Aubery Mendelow's Power–Interest Matrix. It can be used to analyse stakeholders according to whether they have a high or low level of power against a high or low level of interest, in your project or what you are doing. This approach results in the following four segments for stakeholders:

1. *Monitor* for those with low levels of power and low levels of interest in what you are doing or the project.
    *   The approach to take here is a low level of effort and engagement with them.
2. *Keep satisfied* for those with high levels of power and low levels of interest.
    *   Use an approach of meeting their needs and keeping them informed in a way that suits them.

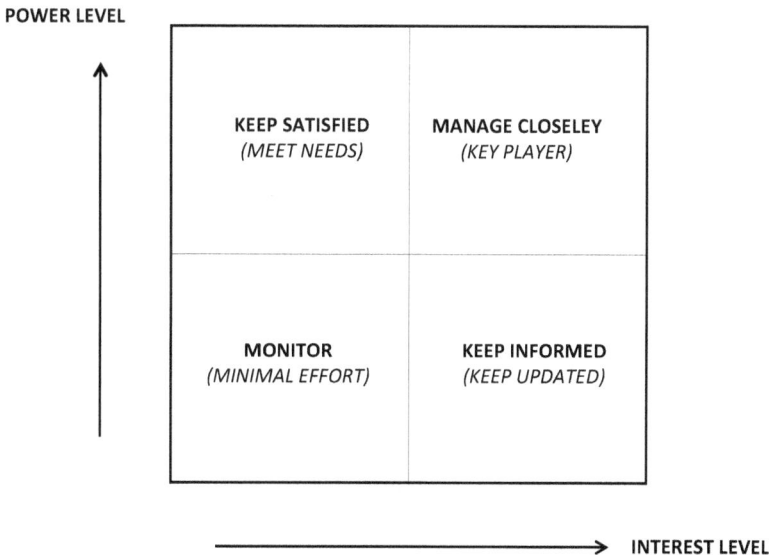

Figure 2.3 Four-box framework for managing stakeholders, based on Mendelow's Power–Interest Matrix (1991)

3. *Keep informed* for people with low levels of power and high levels of interest.
   • Show consideration to them by keeping them updated as they can be potential future advocates.
4. *Manage closely* for key individuals with both high levels of power and high levels of interest.
   • Keep these key players closely informed and engaged, and ensure they are provided with what they need to satisfy them.

Consider Steve from case study B. Where did his digital colleague, Kwame, sit on the Power–Interest Matrix? Initially, because Steve was more senior to Kwame, he believed Kwame had a low level of power and that his instructions would be followed. However, he found Kwame had the authority to control when work was completed. Using the Power–Interest approach, he reassessed Kwame's level of power as high because he prioritised the digital update timings, and his interest level as low because he wasn't interested in Kwame's work. Resulting in a keep-satisfied categorisation where he needed to take the approach of meeting Kwame's needs. By talking to Kwame about his preferred approach to receiving web change requests, Steve was able to manage the relationship by providing overall timelines and the regular detailed email updates Kwame liked to receive to manage his workload.

It is important to note that the category someone is in can quickly change, thus being adaptable and changing approaches is imperative. For example, if your project's accountable executive was in the keep-satisfied box, but something went wrong, they would quickly move to the manage closely box and so it's necessary to adapt your approach accordingly. The matrix particularly helps when reflecting on conflict situations and how to manage them. For example, if you had a conflict where a stakeholder was in the keep informed box because they were very interested in your project, but they had low power or influence to make a decision, you would weigh up how much impact their disagreement would have on the overall outcome of the project and approach this accordingly.

The stakeholder mapping exercise introduced in Chapter 1 provides a practical approach to how to develop relationships with each stakeholder. This, coupled with an analysis of individuals according to Mendalow's Power–Interest Matrix, can be transposed into a stakeholder plan. An example is provided in Table 2.1 which has been populated with two of Steve's relevant stakeholders from case study B.

Table 2.1 Example of a stakeholder plan

Stakeholder	Key interest or issue	Additional info	Power/Interest	How to communicate	Frequency
David – Digital content change manager	Prioritisation and implementation of digital content changes	Has X stakeholders so need to build relationship with him	Keep Satisfied (meet needs)	• Provide timelines • Email status updates • Telephone urgent requests	• Monthly • Weekly • Ad hoc
Product area Y owner	Be aware of the timelines for changes	Build relationships as may need to influence to accommodate urgent changes	Monitor (minimal effort)	• Catch up meeting • Email of timelines • Telephone urgent requests	• Quarterly • Monthly • Ad hoc

A stakeholder plan does not need to have these exact columns and they can be adapted for your workplace. It is just a working tool that enables you to manage stakeholders according to their interest in your work. Mapping their position in terms of power and interest can provide ideas on how to communicate with them, for example, via email or meetings or the level of information they require.

Summary

The suggested practical tools in this chapter support exploring conflict at work. Like with all models, concepts, and approaches, they do not have to be used in their entirety when reflecting or working through conflict. Drawing on relevant elements from them, as required and when useful, can be the key to helping choose the most effective and positive approaches to conflict at work.

Key takeaways

- **Stage**: Identify which stage the conflict is at.
- **Type**: Know what the conflict is actually about.
- **Preference:** Consider which preference approaches to choose when managing the conflict.
- **Power:** Manage stakeholders as they hold the power.

Reflective exercise

1. Think of an example of when you've had a conflict at work and reflect on the stages and type of conflict it was.
2. What is your natural preference style of managing conflict? Use examples of previous conflicts to help you see any patterns.
3. Think of a particular project or piece of work you currently have and construct your stakeholder map.
4. What other key takeaways do you have from this chapter?

References

De Dreu, CKW, van Dierendonck, D, and Dijkstra, MTM (2004). Conflict at work and individual well-being. *International Journal of Conflict Management*, Vol 15, No 1. pp. 6–26. Available at: https://0-doi-org.pugwash.lib.warwick.ac.uk/10.1108/eb022905 (accessed 13 October 2023).

Gallo, A (2017). *HBR Guide to Dealing with Conflict (HBR Guide Series)*. Harvard Business Review Press. Available at: https://ebookcentral.proquest.com/lib/warw/detail.action?docID=5182615 (accessed 16 October 2023).

Kerman, K, Roman, P, Kubicek, B, Meyer, E, Tement, S, and Korunka, C (2022). Conflict at work impairs physiological recovery during Sleep: A daily diary study. *International Journal of Environmental Research and Public Health*. Available at: https://doi.org/10.3390/ijerph191811457 (accessed 16 October 2023).

Mendelow, AL (1991). Environmental scanning: The impact of the stakeholder concept. In *Proceedings from the Second International Conference on Information Systems*, Cambridge, MA.

Pondy, LR (September 1967). Organizational conflict: Concepts and models. *Administrative Science Quarterly*, Vol 12, No 2, pp. 296–320.

Thomas, KW, and Kilmann, RH (1974). *Thomas–Kilmann Conflict Mode Instrument (TKI)*. APA PsycTests. Available at: https://doi.org/10.1037/t02326-000 (accessed 16 October 2023).

PART 2

3

YOU AND YOURSELF

Introduction

This chapter deals with inner conflict experienced either directly in the workplace or as a consequence of something work-related. Inner conflict is the turmoil that happens within yourself, which usually arises from tensions between what you want to do versus what you have to do. Exploring this will make it easier to understand why you may feel or react in a certain way, and appreciate how others may face similar challenges. Often, people get caught in unresolved or toxic stages of the Healthy Conflict Triangle introduced in Chapter 1. This can damage their self-worth and negatively impact their mental health and wellbeing. In this chapter, I introduce some simple positive approaches to navigate and address your own inner conflict or to help others with theirs.

Exploring inner conflict

Inner conflict occurs within you and can create an internal battle as you struggle to resolve it. It can occur within anyone and can be repeated if it is

DOI: 10.4324/9781041056461-5

not managed, resulting in unintended consequences on mental health and wellbeing, such as depression or neurosis. There are times when therapy or counselling may be required, and you can refer to medical healthcare providers for more information.

At work, if inner conflict is not effectively addressed, it can have ramifications on the team or project or organisation, or hinder optimal performance. This can result in less collaboration as relationships are impacted, reduced productivity and lower morale or motivation at work. To gain insight into how inner conflict occurs, a psychological perspective is useful. By understanding how emotions and feelings impact us, we can start to see how this influences cognition and behaviour. Emotions are the raw reactions felt in the body, that usually arise before feelings and they come and go quickly. Feelings are influenced by emotions, experienced within the mind and can last longer. When looking at inner conflict from a psychology perspective, the clash of thoughts and emotions against beliefs and values, results in competing internal desires, goals and dilemmas. The Internal Conflict Model by Toru Sato provides an explanation of this.

> When something is consistent with our desires, we feel comfortable. When something is inconsistent with our desires, we feel anxiety. Therefore, internal conflict can be conceptualized using two constructs: (a) what we desire and (b) what has, is, or could happen. When what we desire matches what has, is, or could happen, we feel comfortable. When what we desire does not match what has, is, or could happen, we feel anxiety.
>
> (Sato, 2005, p. 34)

So, when things go against our desires, it's uncomfortable. The natural tendency is to ease the level of discomfort. Some manage this with unhelpful coping mechanisms to protect themselves, such as filtering what they want to believe, delaying or avoiding thinking or dealing with the situation. However, the risks of continuously doing this can lead to formed habits which make it harder to address the root causes of the inner conflict.

Recognising when there is inner conflict

How can you be more aware of what is going on within yourself, or others? Recognising and being aware of issues before they spiral out of control is important. Using emotions and feelings, we can apply Figure 2.1 to see which stage the inner conflict is at. The emergence of emotions can be a signal of the pre-conflict stage. As feelings develop and cause discomfort, the during-conflict stage takes hold. In the post-conflict stage, particularly if there has been unresolved or toxic inner conflict, lingering feelings can continue and further emotions may arise when reminded of the inner conflict. To further understand why particular emotions or feelings arise, it can be helpful to look at values and behaviours.

Values

Values are basic and fundamental beliefs used to guide how you feel or behave. Often likened to a guiding moral compass. I think of values as what defines and dictates who I am and how I behave. Alternative ways of defining values include:

- The beliefs people have, especially about what is right and wrong and what is most important in life, that control their behaviour.

(Cambridge Dictionary)

- The moral principles and beliefs or accepted standards of a person or social group.

(Collins Dictionary)

Identifying your list of values is a useful exercise you might like to try. Initially, try not to look at a list of values so as not to be swayed towards words that may not be of most importance to you. Sometimes identifying the first few comes quickly, or one value may connect to another that is more relevant. It can help to think about times when you were most happy, fulfilled, or energised, and why this was the case. For example, someone may feel proud they got a promotion because improvement or personal growth were two of their values. Thinking about times of sadness, anger, or irritation can highlight values too. For example, someone could feel disappointed in themselves for sending an email with a spelling mistake, because perfection was one of their values. Sometimes values surface at the most random of times, such as when you are late for a meeting and start feeling flustered, because professionalism or punctuality are your values.

If you struggle to identify your values, there are numerous online resources and a useful one I use with clients aligns with the workplace and is provided by Indeed (2023), '84 Types of values in the workplace (and

Table 3.1 Adapted from '84 types of values in the workplace', Indeed (2023)

BEHAVIOURAL	INTERPERSONAL	SOCIAL	BUSINESS	CULTURAL
1. Independence	16. Trust	32. Responsibility	50. Innovation	67. Inclusion
2. Commitment	17. Humility	33. Accountability	51. Competition	68. Fun
3. Consistency	18. Politeness	34. Environmentalism	52. Leadership	69. Balance
4. Authenticity	19. Leadership	35. Equality	53. Creativity	70. Empowerment
5. Honesty	20. Recognition	36. Diversity	54. Passion	71. Development
6. Bravery	21. Tolerance	37. Globalism	55. Growth	72. Family
7. Loyalty	22. Openness	38. Fairness	56. Resilience	73. Openness
8. Kindness	23. Diversity	39. Objectivity	57. Change	74. Equality
9. Reliability	24. Positivity	40. Localism	58. Improvement	75. Teamwork
10. Spontaneity	25. Candor	41. Merit	59. Collaboration	76. Professionalism
11. Compassion	26. Connectedness	42. Citizenship	60. Excellence	77. Selflessness
12. Enthusiasm	27. Collaboration	43. Freedom	61. Flexibility	78. Productivity
13. Respect	28. Generosity	44. Justice	62. Transparency	79. Efficiency
14. Pragmatism	29. Communication	45. Patriotism	63. Quality	80. Comfort
15. Frugality	30. Humour	46. Altruism	64. Service	81. Celebration
	31. Accessibility	47. Stewardship	65. Ownership	82. Accountability
		48. Respect	66. Expertise	83. Connection
		49. Equity		84. Motivation

how to choose)'. They categorise values into behavioural, interpersonal, social, business, and cultural.

There are many other values not identified in lists you may come up with. Values don't have to be one word, they can be short phrases, for example, *unconditional positive regard*, a value most coaches have.

Behaviours

Behaviours are responses or actions to something which could be internal stimuli such as a thought, or feeling, or external stimuli such as another person. Behaviours can be driven by personality types and various tools that identify natural preferences, such as Myers-Briggs Type Indicator, Hogan Personality Inventory, DiSC, or Spotlight Profiling to name a few, are available. So you can find out more, their websites are included in this chapter's reference section. You may see some people use their personality profiling results as an excuse to behave in a certain way, or to rationalise or excuse their behaviour. For example, when there is a need to make a quick decision, someone who is comfortable working in the detail may rationalise that more time is needed as they are logical and thorough. This could be their unhealthy coping mechanism used to ignore their own inner conflict of moving from the comfort of taking time to switch their behaviour to quick decision-making. Being aware of your preferences and how you naturally behave in both normal and stressful situations, can help you control or adapt the type of behaviour you choose to exhibit.

Being in tune with your values and how they influence behaviour makes it easier to identify the conflict stage. When you anticipate something may contradict your values or cause you to behave in a manner not how you'd like to, this is the pre-conflict stage. As something is going against your values and you've started to behave negatively, the inner conflict unfolds, making this the during-conflict stage. The post-conflict stage comes when the situation concludes when you have recognised that your behaviour was not aligned with your authentic and typical approach because your values had been compromised. Inner conflict may still linger as you deal with the situation's aftermath.

How inner conflict can manifest

We've gone through some of the influences of inner conflict which stem from values and behaviours. We now explore how inner conflict can manifest when faced with challenging situations.

Rationalising

When something happens and aligns with someone's values, this can result in positive feelings which drive their behaviours. Conversely, when something goes against their values, it may trigger negative feelings of anger, sadness or frustration and this also drives their behaviour. Cognitive dissonance theory was explained by Leon Festinger (1957) where he looked at consistency through to inconsistency of what people know or believe and what they actually do. Consider a scenario where someone has been told that to get promoted their visibility must be increased. However, a lack of confidence or the feeling of being exposed leads someone to prefer to remain under the radar. Despite the awareness that more exposure is needed, rationalisation occurs as the person justifies avoiding getting into the spotlight, because it goes against their value of humbleness. This can lead to further rationalisation as they try to believe that promotion will happen by working harder or going over and above what's expected. Justifications of behaviour are used to ensure consistency in behaviour, protecting from perceived inconsistency. Festinger terms inconsistency as dissonance and consistency as consonance with his basic hypotheses:

> 1. The existence of dissonance, being psychologically uncomfortable, will motivate the person to try to reduce the dissonance and achieve consonance.
>
> 2. When dissonance is present, in addition to trying to reduce it, the person will actively avoid situations and information which would likely increase the dissonance.
>
> (Festinger, 1957, p. 3)

CASE STUDY C

Patrick and hybrid working

During the COVID-19 pandemic, Patrick's organisation adopted a 100 per cent work-from-home rule. Responsible for three teams of 20 colleagues, he found leading them extremely difficult during this period. He believed being in the office was the best way to ensure they were productive and to keep an eye on them. He felt he lost control which caused him to micro-manage his team and their work by implementing more meetings and daily email updates to check they were doing what they should be. This resulted in increasing his and their workload which impacted their morale.

Patrick initially experienced cognitive dissonance because his belief that people should be in the office to work effectively, clashed against the organisation's new policy of working from home due to external conditions. To reduce his level of cognitive dissonance, he had introduced new working norms such as more update meetings and emails, to justify his belief that this would ensure his team was still productive. Thus, maintaining a sense of consistency with his beliefs.

Procrastination

Inner conflict can also manifest through delaying or postponing tasks, known as procrastination. Often procrastination can be seen as laziness, however, usually underlying factors can be the cause, such as lack of confidence or lack of ability. Feeling overwhelmed is common when there are difficult tasks, and distraction is used by completing simpler tasks to avoid the more difficult ones. The problem with procrastination is it can form into a habit which requires effort to break.

CASE STUDY D

Leng, the 'Procrastination Queen'

Leng had labelled herself the 'Procrastination Queen'. She worked in a fast-paced organisation where speed was a key value. Responsible for an important project, she found herself not focusing on it. She knew there were a number of different workstreams to get a grip of, but the tasks kept circling in her mind. Her line manager had been waiting for an update, but as he trusted her capabilities and liked to provide autonomy to his team, assumed all was in hand. Leng would plan what to do, but kept replanning and not putting anything into action. Upon reflection during coaching, she realised she tended to do this with big tasks as she preferred to tick smaller tasks off her list, to feel a sense of achievement. She found the scale and significance of the project daunted her and felt overwhelmed. She didn't want her line manager to think she couldn't handle it, however, she couldn't surface the clear priorities as she was still working alone, stuck in this inner conflict. Fear of failing made her anxious and her coping mechanism was distracting herself with other simpler tasks such as emails or meetings. With this project, she was already late and at risk of not meeting the deadline.

Leng was caught up with inner conflict and used procrastination to avoid going on, flipping between the unresolved and toxic stages of her inner conflict. The anxiety she felt was evident as she was losing sleep (toxic stage). At other times she ignored the situation by distracting herself with less important tasks (unresolved stage). Once she identified what was stopping her from moving forward, she was able to talk to her line manager to gain support. By explaining all her planned options, he supported her to find the best way forward. Due to her procrastination, the project was delivered late, but she used the learning as a reminder of how to identify the stage of inner conflict early. She now calls herself the 'Procrastination Princess', as she still has a tendency to start procrastinating, but can identify the conflict stage earlier now which helps her address it.

Examples of inner conflict

Cognitive distortion refers to the way people may think of or perceive information about themselves which may not align with reality. These thoughts or ways of thinking can have a negative impact on mental health and wellbeing. At work, inner conflict can often stem from cognitive distortions and here are some common examples you might identify with or have seen in others you work with.

Imposter syndrome

Imposter syndrome is when someone has feelings of inadequacy, undeserving success or recognition, despite being successful at what they do. Clients often say they are afraid of being found out or feeling like a fraud, and downplay their achievements or success. A Harvard Business Review article, 'You're not an imposter. You're actually pretty amazing', by Kess Eruteya (2022), says about 70 per cent of people experience imposter syndrome at some point. Many high achievers experience self-doubt or lack confidence in themselves, and this can manifest quickly when starting new roles or in new situations with people they've not dealt with before. Even when others sing their praises, they may still feel unworthy.

Fear of failure

Fear of failure can be rooted in upbringing and background, or how failure was dealt with in the past. At work, worrying about making mistakes or wrong decisions is common, which can lead to fewer risks taken, impeding professional growth, or hindering innovation on business projects. This fear can be unfounded, but the potential failure alone can result in avoiding situations and not moving forward.

Limiting beliefs

Limiting beliefs are when thinking and believing something is the absolute truth, stops you from taking action. This can come in the form of over-generalising by labelling yourself as not being able to do something, or fortune-telling where you think you can predict negative outcomes. At work, this could be feeling too young to be a line manager, or too busy for personal development. Some limiting beliefs may stem from backgrounds, and overcoming these can cause inner conflict, particularly when they contradict your values. For example, if you're asked to quickly deliver a minimum viable proposition (something that fulfils just the essential requirements to be delivered to market) at work, but this goes against your values of quality and perfectionism.

Developing skills

Thinking that you cannot develop a new skill or enhance an existing one can cause inner conflict, especially if the job or project requires it. It may feel that the gap between where you are now to where you need to be is too wide and unachievable. The Zone of Proximal Development (ZPD) by Vygotsky (1978) can be a useful concept to reflect on in these circumstances. Vygotsky's theories are based on three modes of learning which are cognitive, motoric, and sociocultural:

- Cognitive learning is thinking about how ideas can be used.
- Motoric learning is about doing things in practice such as being hands-on.
- Sociocultural learning focuses on a collaborative and supportive approach with others.

The ZPD is when and where support from others is required for progress. Another of his ideas, the More Knowledgeable Other (MKO), is someone who knows about what is trying to be developed or learnt. Thus, acquiring a new skill with relevant support from an MKO can enable someone to learn in the ZPD.

Inner conflict can arise if people think they are unable to develop the skill, may not identify they need help, or may be reluctant to ask for support. Some may think they can master the skill without support and this can also cause inner conflict when they struggle or fail. Recognising and acknowledging when help is required and seeking support from an MKO enables you to move from being unable to do it on your own, into the ZPD of being able to do it with help, and ultimately being able to do it independently.

Common work-related examples could be the fear of public speaking, presenting in meetings, voicing ideas, or technical skills. For example, a new team member who has not used a particular application before may be embarrassed to admit they don't know how to use it and will be unable to do it on their own. However, with a little support from an MKO such as a peer or an alternative method of finding support, such as via an internet search, they can move into the ZPD, learning how to do some basic things in the application with the support. Then they could move into being able

Zone of Proximal Development

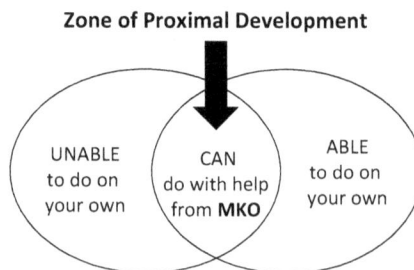

Figure 3.1 Adapted from Zone of Proximal Development, Vygotsky (1978)

to learn on their own, as they have some familiarity with the application and build on this independently. Perhaps, you've experienced something yourself or noticed one of your team who you've been trying to persuade to do something but they are still reluctant to do so. Asking for support or providing it to another person can help people move forward and develop new skills.

Personal versus professional brand

The terms personal brand and professional brand are used interchangeably, and both point to your reputation or what you are known in the workplace. Here, they will be treated slightly differently as it helps with understanding and managing inner conflict. I liken a personal brand to how someone is outside work, and it encompasses personality, values, interests and passions. With professional brand it is about how someone is at work and also includes skills, expertise and experience. These can both be different, however often there is overlap as personal brand feeds into how people are at work. Sometimes, people experience inner conflict due to the incongruence of how they are outside and inside work. Have you ever felt you cannot be your authentic self at work? Maybe there are elements of you, you've felt you cannot show. Some are totally different people at home and at work. The differences can be further exacerbated by the culture of the team or organisation, for example, misalignment of values, or professional expectations versus personal goals. This can be seen when people are expected to take on promotions with more pressure and responsibility, which goes against their personal goals of not desiring this. Inner conflict arises as they are torn between what's expected and what they want. Even managing perceptions of how people see you against how you actually are, can cause inner conflict. Trying to uphold the professional brand people expect while trying to remain authentic to you can become unsustainable.

Practical positive approaches to get to healthy inner conflict

We have covered how values can drive behaviours and when inner conflict situations arise how we rationalise what is happening. Regardless of what the inner conflict is, there are some ways to approach any of the pre-, during-, and post-inner conflict. Getting to healthy conflict is the aim and some positive approaches to this can help you with your own inner conflict or to support other people such as a colleague or member of your team. Please be aware that if there are deeper psychological factors at play, it may be appropriate to seek professional support. These approaches are primarily for those who want to manage the inner conflict themselves.

STOP!

Whichever inner conflict stage you are at, intentionally pausing the situation provides a space for you to take a closer examination of what is going on. It's helpful to stop, and then confirm your intention to work through your inner conflict. This deliberate reminder will enable you to step back from the immediate turbulence you are experiencing. For some, especially pro-crastinators, this may be the most difficult thing to do. However, stopping provides a way to interrupt and break the automatic cycle of inner conflict you may be in, to work it through. This is not about avoiding the conflict, it's about breaking the unhealthy inner conflict that is being experienced.

Reflect on where you are

There may be tension or unease within you and as soon as you notice this, remind yourself to take that pause to stop, to reflect on what is happening regarding your values and behaviours. Notice at which stage the inner conflict is at (pre-, during-, or post-). By reminding yourself of your values or any personality profiling you've had, begin to note your behaviours. At this point, acknowledge what is really happening. This can be a tricky task as sometimes what you want to believe is taking place, may not be what is actually happening. Try to focus on the facts and be honest with yourself. The inner conflict may be due to a result of distortion of what is actually happening.

Don't make it personal

A pragmatic way to approach this is to take the personal part out of it. Of course, it is personal to you, but being objective or detaching yourself from the inner conflict, can be a positive way that enables a realistic and factual view of the situation. If you find this challenging, imagine transferring your inner conflict to another person, and imagine none of it is happening to you. Then ask them what is actually going on, and respond as though you are the other person. This will enable you to think less emotionally about it and provide different perspectives on the situation.

Voice it out or write it down

Another way to express facts is to say it out loud or write it down. More clarity surfaces when things are transferred from within the mind out into the open. It encourages you to articulate and make sense of what is happening. Some find journaling a way of getting thoughts out. I personally find this useful, especially when my thoughts go around and around and I get nowhere. As I can journal for long lengths of time, I set a ten-minute boundary to focus and get the key issues that bother me. Sometimes, this is all that's needed to get over the inner conflict and move on. It can also provide clarity on what the key issues are so I can then start to address them.

Reassess the inner conflict

Now that the facts of what is happening may be clearer, you will know what is causing the inner conflict. Have you ever been told to develop a skill that you've been reluctant to do? I remember my line manager repeatedly telling me to get closer to the numbers. Internally, I blamed myself for wanting this commercial role knowing I was not a numbers person. This went on for six months and I was getting further and further away from the numbers and focusing on any activity that did not involve them. It took a year-end review for me to stop and take a good look at what was happening. I realised the inner conflict I experienced wasn't due to whether or not I should have the job, or whether I was capable. It took me back to when I was an investment analyst trying to number crunch my way through complex forecasting without the technical skills to do so. I reassessed what getting closer to the numbers meant and reframed the situation.

Reframe and shift perspective

Once the truth or what is deemed as the truth has been drawn out, look objectively at it. Take each point and reframe what could be happening in a different or positive way. This shifts your perspective. Take Leng's example, when she delivered the project late, this caused another round of inner conflict as she blamed herself for not getting it started earlier due to her procrastination. By reframing this to see that it was delivered and that her line manager was supportive of the approach taken, she was able to shift her perspective to remind herself to seek support when needed in the future.

Fear setting

On occasions, fear holds people back from working through what is going on. Tim Ferriss (2017) delivered a TED Talk on a technique called fear setting and defining fears. Inner conflict is often due to fear, and focusing on two parts of his technique can help: (i) defining your fears and (ii) thinking about how to prevent them. Listing fears relating to the inner conflict helps surface what is worrying you, so you can start to think about addressing them. Often, fear warps what is going on and causes you to exaggerate negative consequences or understate any positive results. Fear risks leading to no action. If I'd asked myself his two questions and applied them to my inner conflict of getting closer to the numbers, it might have looked like this.

- Define the worst-case scenario or what could go wrong: (1) I can't build accurate Excel models; (2) I produce the wrong answers and wrong decisions will be made resulting in commercial loss; and (3) I will be found out that I am not right for the job.
- How I could prevent this: (1) learn to build Excel models or collaborate with someone who can such as the finance team; (2) ask the finance team to check my workings or collaborate with the finance team to make commercial decisions; (3) getting closer to the numbers does not have to mean number crunching, reframe it as understanding the numbers to drive the business.

What's the worst that can happen?

Resilience is the ability to bounce back from adversity and during times of inner conflict, this may feel difficult as it can be hard to reframe or shift perspectives because negative outcomes are focused on. Have you ever made a mistake at work and immediately thought you were going to be sacked? This jump to the worst possible outcome is known as catastrophising. To gain perspective, a simple technique a colleague shared with me is to put your hand out with open fingers and identify the worst possible thing that can happen and apply it to your thumb. Next, go to your little finger to identify the best thing that can happen. Then for the fingers in between, think of some middle-ground results. The likelihood is that the worst and best may not happen, and it's likely something in between will. In my case of the numbers, the worst thing that could have happened was being managed out of the team, the best thing was that I would be a commercial expert at number crunching, but somewhere in between I would be able to develop a level of commercial ability that would be right for the job to persuade my line manager that I was closer to the numbers.

Plan what you want to happen

Once you have stopped, reflected and reassessed your inner conflict, there is the need to do something about it. This is where the real struggle can come as it is much easier to delay, ignore or think it is too late to do anything. Regardless of which stage the conflict is at, there is still merit in dealing with it and this means planning what you do to make the change happen to stop the inner conflict.

Engage a growth mindset

Once you notice the inner conflict, believing that something can be done about it is key. This is where Carol Dweck's (2006) concept of a growth mindset comes in handy. In her research she found those who believe change or improvement can happen, are able to cultivate a growth mindset where challenges are embraced, obstacles are worked through, feedback or criticism is learnt from, and with hard work change happens. Compared with a fixed mindset where the belief is that abilities and intelligence cannot be changed or improved, which can lead to challenges being avoided. Here are a couple of examples of how inner conflict situations can be seen differently by switching from a fixed to a growth mindset and changing the inner voice. This provides an approach to aid reflection and to reassess the situation, producing actions on how to move forward.

Table 3.2 Examples of inner conflict with fixed and growth mindsets

Inner Conflict Example	Fixed Mindset	Growth Mindset
Wanting a promotion, but not being confident enough to apply for them when they arise. Gets frustrated with himself as colleagues move on.	• I don't have the skills, knowledge, or experience for the job. • I can't leave my team, they need me and it would be embarrassing if I don't get it.	➤ I will gain experience by addressing the gaps with stretch projects. ➤ I will focus on developing a culture of development, upskilling my team, and building a succession plan.
Not happy with hybrid working and prefers to work from home all the time.	• The team will distract me, I focus better alone without others talking to me. • The commute will waste my time.	➤ I can learn from water cooler chats, especially with colleagues from other teams. ➤ I can use the commute time to listen to podcasts or catch up on news.

Focus on solutions, not problems

Think of actions that can be done to solve or address parts of the inner conflict. This can transform thinking as the focus is shifted to what can be done instead of remaining stuck on the problem. Setting goals using frameworks such as SMART or CLEAR goals can help to break down and scope out what can be done.

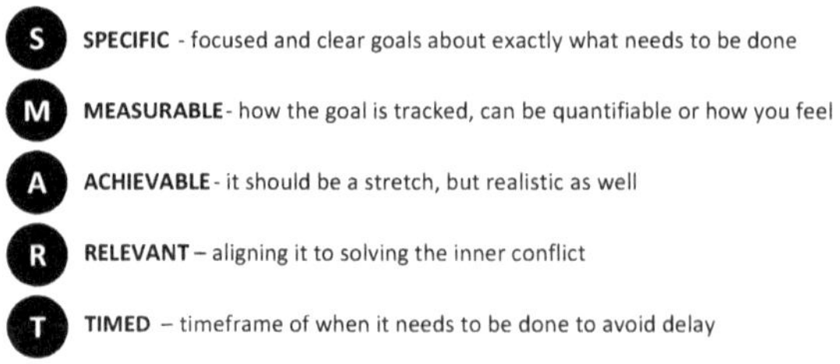

S SPECIFIC - focused and clear goals about exactly what needs to be done

M MEASURABLE - how the goal is tracked, can be quantifiable or how you feel

A ACHIEVABLE - it should be a stretch, but realistic as well

R RELEVANT – aligning it to solving the inner conflict

T TIMED – timeframe of when it needs to be done to avoid delay

Figure 3.2 SMART goals

For example, when using SMART, instead of focusing on the problem of not getting promoted, switch to a goal that focuses on what can be done to achieve a promotion, such as:

- Specific – Get promoted to [job title] in the [department] through developing leadership skills by volunteering to work on stretch projects outside of the team.
- Measurable – Successfully lead on one stretch project every quarter, seeking feedback from the line manager and senior stakeholders on a monthly basis.
- Achievable – Proactively seek opportunities to lead other projects by asking the line manager and senior stakeholders to ensure the relevant projects are appropriately set up for my involvement.
- Relevant – Choose the stretch projects that will support the development of my leadership skills.
- Timely – Complete [x] stretch projects by [date].

CLEAR can be applied to the same example.

- Collaborate – Work with line manager and senior stakeholders to identify appropriate stretch projects outside of my team.
- Limited scope – Focus on successfully leading one stretch project every quarter and receiving positive feedback on leadership skills of influencing and driving change.
- Emotional – Maintain a growth mindset, acknowledge challenges and seek support from the line manager when inner conflict arises.

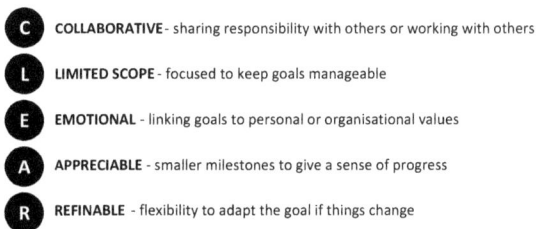

C **COLLABORATIVE** - sharing responsibility with others or working with others

L **LIMITED SCOPE** - focused to keep goals manageable

E **EMOTIONAL** - linking goals to personal or organisational values

A **APPRECIABLE** - smaller milestones to give a sense of progress

R **REFINABLE** - flexibility to adapt the goal if things change

Figure 3.3 CLEAR goals

- Appreciable – Start with a first stretch project and gain feedback from stakeholders on progress and development of leadership skills before taking on another project.
- Refinable – Be adaptable to refine approach from feedback and realistically access additional projects against workload.

Either of these practical approaches provides a tangible way to reframe problems into solutions with a systematic way to achieve them. Goals are important to help move forward, however, what's also important is how solutions are focused on as a way of resolving inner conflict.

Engage support from others

The approaches provided are useful when dealing with inner conflict by yourself. However, there are times when it may be helpful to seek support from others. These can be in the form of professionals such as a coach or mentor, and part three of this book provides more information. There can also be value in discussing inner conflict with a range of people.

- **Personal friends or significant other.** These people may be a little biased in that they may agree with your version of what is happening, resulting in collusion which can exacerbate the inner conflict. They may also challenge and disagree which may add to your emotional wellbeing. Being clear on why you want to discuss will frame what you get out of the conversation. For example, you may just want to rant or get everything out needing a listening ear. Or perhaps you want advice and if they give it, be ready for what they say as you may not agree with it. Take care not to overburden these people as it can impact their mental health and wellbeing as they have a personal vested interest in you.
- **Line manager.** If you trust your line manager and have a space of psychological safety, you may find it useful to talk to them. Even if you don't, consider how to approach them with your issues as their role is to support you. They have the responsibility to ensure their team is doing OK and can often bring a different perspective or alleviate your worries altogether. They are there to prioritise, open doors and help you do your job more effectively. Not all line managers behave this

way, and you will be aware of your individual situation. If you are a line manager, supporting your team members with their own inner conflict is important and noticing when they may be in these situations can be a chance to invite them to discuss their inner conflict with you.

• **Work friends or other colleagues.** Here, choosing the right type of person is key. Perhaps seek out the mind openers who can enable you to unlock other perspectives or energisers to boost your motivation to work through your inner conflict. Navigators can provide guidance on how to approach things too. Try not to use them to rant or download as this is not an effective use of their time.

Summary

The suggested approaches to managing inner conflict are some practical methods to deal with inner conflict at work. What you use on yourself or with members of your team will be dependent on the situation. Having the foundation of working through inner conflict will support how you deal with other conflict situations and will be built on throughout other chapters.

Key takeaways

• Values and behaviours are key drivers that impact inner conflict.
• Work provides a broad range of reasons that cause inner conflict.
• Inner conflict can manifest negatively if not acknowledged and addressed and it's crucial to stop, reflect, reassess, and replan what you can do to address it.
• Adopting a positive approach to handling inner conflict will help manage it.

Reflective exercise

1. Think of a situation when you've had an inner conflict at work and reflect on how you handled the situation.
2. List your top six values and prioritise them in order of importance and then do the following:
   a. Identify if any of your values were compromised in the inner conflict situation identified in question 1.

      b.   How did it make you feel, what emotions did you experience?

      c.   What behaviours did this lead to?

3.   Which approaches explored in this chapter could you have used to address the inner conflict from question 1?

4.   What other key takeaways do you have from this chapter?

References

Conte, B, Hahnel, UJJ, and Brosch, T (2023). From values to emotions: Cognitive appraisal mediates the impact of core values on emotional experience. *Emotion*, Vol 23, No 4, pp. 1115–1129. Available at: https://doi.org/10.1037/emo0001083.

Cambridge Dictionary (nd). Available at: https://dictionary.cambridge.org/dictionary/english/values (accessed 6 November 2023).

Collins Dictionary (nd). Available at: www.collinsdictionary.com/dictionary/english/values (accessed 6 November 2023).

DiSC Profile (nd). Available at : www.discprofile.com.

Dweck, C (2006). *Mindset*. The Random House Publishing Group.

Ferriss, T (2017). Why you should define your fears instead of your goals. *TED*. Available at: https://www.ted.com/talks/tim_ferriss_why_you_should_define_your_fears_instead_of_your_goals?language=en, (accessed 8 November 2023).

Festinger, L (1957). *A Theory of Cognitive Dissonance*. Stanford University Press.

Eruteya, K (2022). You're not an imposter. You're actually pretty amazing. *Harvard Business Review*. Available at: https://hbr.org/2022/01/youre-not-an-imposter-youre-actually-pretty-amazing?registration=success (accessed 7 November 2023).

Hogan (nd). Available at: www.hoganassessments.com.

Indeed (2023). 84 Types of values in the workplace (and how to choose them). *Indeed*. Available at: https://www.indeed.com/career-advice/career-development/types-of-values (accessed 6 November 2023).

Sato, T (2005). The internal conflict model: A theoretical framework for integration. *The Humanistic Psychologist*, Vol 33, No 1, pp. 33–44. https://doi.org/10.1207/s15473333thp3301_4.

Spotlight Profiling (nd). Available at: www.mindflick.co.uk.

The Myers-Briggs Company (nd). Available at: www.themyersbriggs.com

Vygotsky, LS (1978). *Mind in Society: The Development of Higher Psychological Processes*. Harvard University Press.

4

YOU AND ANOTHER

Introduction

This chapter covers conflict occurring between two individuals at work, referred to here as two-party conflict. It may be that you are one of the people involved in the conflict, or you are neither of those two people and you notice two others involved in a conflict that impacts your work, team or organisation. Often, two-party conflict just requires the opening up of communication, however, it's not always that simple. A multi-faceted approach may be required to address misunderstandings, unmet expectations, differing values, power dynamics, or external influences that might complicate getting to healthy conflict or resolution. Here, we explore different types of two-party conflict that commonly occur at work together with some positive approaches you can use to manage this yourself. There may be times when it's more effective to engage a third party to help, such as a workplace mediator, and instances of when this can be effective and what it entails is covered in Chapter 9.

DOI: 10.4324/9781041056461-6

Exploring two-party conflict

At work, different types of relationships are required and these can be within a team, across different teams, or within a hierarchy chain of command. Further variations of relationships are found in matrix organisations where there are vertical and horizontal responsibilities across functions and business units, additional dotted line reporting to more than one leader and pan-organisational projects. There are also external relationships such as those with clients or customers, consumer groups, suppliers, regulators, government bodies or the media. The example stakeholder map shown in Chapter 1's Figure 1.1 depicts over 30 different stakeholder relationships, and yours may be even more far-reaching. With all these stakeholder interactions, it's likely conflict, no matter how small or big, will arise at some

Table 4.1 Example of types of two-party relationships

Co-workers or peers	When working alongside others, particularly within the same team, wider team, or the same office space, disagreements often occur. There will be a mix of personalities, interests, and values to contend with, along with the challenges and influences that come with work such as deadlines and resource constraints.
Line manager and direct report	Conflict between line managers and direct reports is common throughout a working relationship. You may be a line manager, a direct report, or both, navigating how to work up and down within the hierarchy.
Interdepartmental	Working with people across teams comes into play when on projects, or if you are on a leadership team working with leaders from different units or functions. Friction can also occur if you have a dotted line reporting to someone in another business unit or function, or if someone has a dotted line to you, as two different teams' priorities compete against each other.
Clients or customers	Different dynamics contribute to conflict that arises when working with clients or customers. Often, clients expect to have the upper hand with 'the customer is always right' being a universal phrase. However there will be times when the customer is not right, and dealing with this type of conflict can be tricky to balance against business needs.

point. It's even more likely that you're managing different conflicts with different stakeholders at the same time. Table 4.1 shows some of the types of relationships and conflicts experienced at work.

Recognising when there is a two-party conflict

A combination of understanding the healthy conflict triangle (healthy, unresolved and toxic) and stage of conflict categorisation (pre, during and post) from Chapter 2 can help to recognise when there is a two-party conflict.

- In the pre-conflict stage, subtle signs may emerge such as misalignment with values, or potential differences of agendas that may cause disagreement. It can be easy to notice this when in the during-conflict stage as emotions may be high, tension arises, and there may be reduced collaboration. At this stage, toxic conflict can occur, with signs such as deadlock between both parties refusing to back down, or behaviours such as shouting or arguing.
- If both parties ignore, refuse to, or put off dealing with the issue, this can result in unresolved conflict, and there may be an impasse as they are unable to move forward. There might then be a risk of being forced into a position of quickly deciding what to do if time becomes short, which may not result in a good conclusion for the business or project. You may see healthy conflict where there is mutual respect and understanding as both parties work through disagreements in a psychologically safe environment.
- In post-conflict, there may be resolved or unresolved issues, but both parties will have deemed the disagreement as over. However, sometimes the issues rear their head again at a later date and thus can also be deemed as unresolved conflict.

How two-party conflict can manifest

Two-party conflict emerges due to reasons such as work priorities, different perspectives, misunderstandings, power dynamics or communication styles. Gallo's (2017) approach introduced in Chapter 2, is a practical way to ascertain if it's a relationship, task, process or status issue. Some examples of these manifesting are the following:

- **Relationship conflict** is when there are personal or personality differences. It could be where one person is more direct and the other is reflective in communication. This difference in working can snowball every time they have to work together if they don't come up with a collaborative approach that works for both.
- **Task conflict** is when there is disagreement over what the goal is. For example, where an existing service needs to be optimised, and the finance representative wants to prioritise decisions based on cost savings. However, the technology specialist may focus on digitisation and shortening the customer journey which costs more. Both assume optimisation to mean different things and remain focused on their viewpoint which could result in delays in decision-making impacting the project.
- **Process conflict** is where there are differences in how to reach the outcome. An example could be with two colleagues, working on the customer research element of developing a new product, disagreeing on the approach to collect customer insight. One favours a quantitative approach to collecting data via online questionnaires, and the other prefers a qualitative approach using interviews or focus groups. A way of refocusing on the best approach could be to look at the other resource allocations such as time or cost implications to help decide which research approach is more practical.
- **Status conflict** can arise over where people stand in relation to each other. For example, two people from different teams working together want visibility in leading a piece of work. I had a client who had this specific issue which resulted in both he and his colleague constantly competing to provide the lead updates for a weekly communication. It came to a head when the director asked them to provide one coordinated update instead and they had to collaborate and sometimes compromise.

Conflict can manifest in ways which can be difficult to categorise, particularly when underlying issues may stem from a while ago or when minor disagreements accumulate over time.

Repeated conflict

Ongoing conflict grows due to repeated patterns of behaviour or reoc-curring situations. Each instance of conflict can trigger more tension as demonstrated in Figure 4.1. Arguably, irritation and annoyance are simpler to manage and the emotions may be minor and manageable if addressed. People can often avoid addressing the conflict, in the hope that it will resolve itself. As the conflict intensifies and, if not managed, it goes to toxic conflict as anger emerges and it could escalate to violent behaviours which might include verbal abuse or physical harm in extreme circumstances. At this point immediate attention would be required to de-escalate the situ-ation. At the most extreme end, serious consequences such as disciplinary action may be required and this is covered in Chapter 10. Thus, if conflict situations are not addressed, there is a risk they build up and be blown out of proportion. Examples can range from relatively simple social situations such as the colleague shirking their turn of the tea round, to situations impacting the business like the high-value client constantly demanding discounted rates.

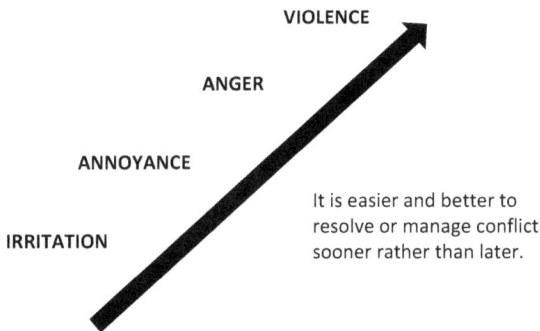

VIOLENCE

ANGER

ANNOYANCE

It is easier and better to
resolve or manage conflict
sooner rather than later.

IRRITATION

Figure 4.1 Levels of conflict

CASE STUDY E

Kai and Maria

Kai was responsible for the quarterly awaydays for his team of 50. It felt like a thankless job, especially because one of his peers, Maria, always had something to say. She was known for being overly critical, a blocker, and never taking ownership. He dreaded this part of his job as her criticisms had gone on for four years, and what began as mild irritation had moved to annoyance and now anger. He considered leaving the team to avoid dealing with her and had coaching to work through his options. He reflected on what he had done previously, which included a team meeting where people could give suggestions, though it was dominated by her, so other colleagues could not input. He had tried asking Maria to help organise them, but she refused. Kai realised he didn't really want to leave, he just wanted to find a way to organise awaydays without feeling angry at what Maria may say. He decided to have a meeting with her so he could be honest about how he felt. Maria was upset because she hadn't realised there was any conflict and was unaware of the impact she had on him and the team. She realised what she thought were helpful suggestions were perceived negatively due to how she communicated. Although their relationship did not improve drastically, they did move into healthy conflict. This type of built-up conflict can often be seen where repeated patterns of behaviour exacerbate the situation into a toxic or unresolved conflict.

Legacy conflict

When things have always been done in a certain way or when people or teams seem bound by their own rules, this can give rise to legacy conflict. Legacy conflict can stem from entrenched practices, beliefs or structures that persist over time. It can also emerge when people cling to established systems, norms, habits or processes. This can be triggered by organisational culture shifts, changes in the team or leadership, resource constraints, etc. Conflict can arise when people do not want to adapt to change and can hinder innovation or create tension. For example:

* A new leader introducing a different strategy which a direct report may not agree with as they are accustomed to the existing strategic direction.
* Long-standing systems owned by a colleague who has a limited budget may result in conflict when a new colleague with more budget suggests radical changes.
* Generational differences between two people can also be a type of legacy conflict due to varying perspectives on working approaches or expectations.

Navigating legacy conflict requires sensitivity and the Power–Interest Matrix in Chapter 2 comes in useful to understand levels of power (or influence) and interest each party has in relation to the conflict. For instance, if one party holds more power, as seen in the example of the colleague responsible for the long-standing system, the other party with more budget may decide to strategically accommodate. They may suggest the need to revisit this in the future using a more collaborative approach, and in the meantime work on building trust to influence them to aim for a mutually beneficial solution. Another example to help illustrate this is with two peers where one is more cautious and the other a risk taker. The latter returns from a course with new ideas they want to implement which the first is reluctant to. Although their power levels are the same, the peer who went on the course has a greater level of interest in making the changes. They could accommodate each other by agreeing a gradual test-and-learn approach of small-scale pilot changes where changes are not implemented until both are comfortable.

With legacy issues, guidelines or rules that are not owned by the two people can cause conflict between them and this can be too challenging for them to resolve and alternative approaches such as escalation may be required.

CASE STUDY F

Kiran and Teejay

Kiran from the brand team had a conflict with Teejay, a new social media manager. Teejay proposed collaborating with an upcoming influencer with a younger target audience. However, Kiran voiced concerns that it didn't align with the brand's traditional image and age segment of the market. Teejay heard from his team that the brand team never allowed anything innovative and always controlled marketing using the argument of protecting the brand. They both had many conversations to try to balance creative needs with brand guidelines. However, eventually both couldn't compromise, and as time was ticking they agreed to escalate the impasse to their line managers. This resulted in a meeting together with their line managers to work on a way forward. Later, when it came to the next review of brand guidelines, Kiran was able to incorporate more detailed social media guidelines for customer segments. Thus the conflict which stemmed from legacy issues, enabled a change in the process moving forward.

Examples of two-party conflict

There are numerous occasions where two-party conflict occurs and sometimes this may be a combination of different influencing factors occurring together, rather than a single cause. Here are some examples you may have seen in the workplace and you may notice more than one of these leading to a conflict you can think of:

- Breakdown in communication leading to misunderstandings, misinformation, or lack of clarity.
- Different performance expectations, management styles, or contrasting work ethics.
- Ambiguous or unclear roles and responsibilities which are not clearly defined or understood.
- Resource constraints such as time, budget, or resources.
- Different goals or objectives, and prioritisation of work.
- Competition for visibility, recognition, or promotion opportunities.
- Ethical dilemmas or cultural differences.

Practical positive approaches to get to healthy conflict

With the assumption that getting to healthy conflict is the best way forward for both parties, there are a number of different approaches that can be used. Often, it takes more than one approach and a combination of them can be more effective because conflict is not straightforward. When two people are involved, posing the question of what is at stake for the project, the team, or the organisation can provide insight into any broader implications. This approach provides a strategic lens to examine what the impact would be if the conflict is not worked through. It encourages different perspectives to be explored, to help uncover what is of most importance when resolving or finding a way through the conflict.

STOP!

As with inner conflict, it is important to stop when you suspect there is a two-party conflict to determine the stage or type of conflict, if not already clarified. It can be difficult to pause to reflect on this, because when emotions and feelings are involved, this is when disagreements with another person can result in strong emotions. This can happen when the Chimp, introduced in Chapter 1, is activated before the Human part of the brain has a chance to kick into rational thinking. During this time strong emotions can arise, for example, in conflict situations, individuals may experience emotions such as anger or defensiveness impacting the ability to collaborate or find a resolution.

> Emotions that simmer beneath the threshold of awareness can have a powerful impact on how we perceive and react ... He may well be oblivious to it, though it stews just out of his awareness and dictates his curt replies. But once that reaction is brought into awareness – once it registers in the cortex – he can evaluate things anew, decide to shrug off the feelings left earlier in the day, and change his outlook and mood.
>
> (Goleman, 1995, p. 55)

Stopping serves as a reminder to pause to create space to determine a considered way forward.

Reflect on where you are both at

Reflection can be challenging as there may be many influencing factors to contend with especially as you are unaware of the challenges or goals the other person has to consider. Likewise, they may not be aware of yours. Notice at which stage the conflict is at (pre-, during-, or post-) and what type of conflict it is (relationship, task, process, or situation). Then ensuring that you have the intention of wanting to do something is key otherwise getting stuck in an unresolved or toxic conflict will happen.

Separate the people from the problem

Not only do you have to contend with your own feelings, but there are those of the other person too. With disagreements, it can be easy to take things personally, on both sides as it may feel like a personal attack that threatens your self-worth. The method of Principled Negotiation is a collaborative approach to negotiation developed by the Havard Negotiation Project (Harvard Business School, 1979), and is set out by Fisher and Ury (1991). Conflict is addressed based on fair standards integrating both parties' interests to get to a mutually beneficial solution. One of the key principles is to separate the people from the problem. As emotions, personalities and egos arise, this focuses people on each other and the relationship between them, rather than the problem itself. They suggest it can be helpful to 'Face the problem, not the people … A more effective way for the parties to think of themselves is as partners in a hardheaded, side-by-side search for a fair agreement advantageous to each other' (Fisher and Ury, 1991, p. 40).

Another way to think about this is to move to an objective stance and this can be done in these two ways.

1. Don't take things personally, because this can negatively impact your mental health and wellbeing. For example, if your colleague was assigned to share responsibility for your project it could cause resent-ment if you think your line manager believes you're not capable of leading it, or perhaps you think your colleague is encroaching on your territory. However, what if your line manager didn't want to over-burden you because he thought you already had a lot of work? There is usually another angle to what is happening and being able to disconnect and by not taking things personally, you may see alternative perspectives.
2. Pragmatically assess what is happening by standing back from the situ-ation similar to the analogy of having a helicopter view. Observing from a third-party perspective can bring to light more information to assess what is going on. This is especially helpful if the situation is indeed personal, for example, if the other person is purposely manipu-lative or controlling.

Detaching yourself or the other person from the conflict can be particularly useful when dealing with task or process issues as well because it enables the focus to be placed back on what the conflict is about so that solutions can be worked through.

Clarify understanding

When there is an issue, no one has to be at fault. There may not be con-sensus about what the conflict is specifically about, and clarifying a rela-tionship, task, process or status conflict through a conversation with both parties can ensure there is an aligned understanding or even a change in your or the other's viewpoint. Broadening how the conflict impacts the project or activity, or the impact on the organisation can be an alternative perspectives to use. Organisations have their own culture or way of doing things, and some articulate it by using terms such as company values or guiding principles to focus employees on what is important, which can be used to focus conflict outcomes too.

Plan what you want to happen

To move forward, a plan of action is essential and this can be done by either party or both together. This involves thinking of the options that can be adopted and having the intention to do something about it otherwise the conflict will not be resolved or move to a healthy conflict. Working on solutions and not the problems provides a practical approach to solving the issue, using frameworks or approaches introduced in the previous chapter such as SMART goals. However, sometimes it may not be as straightforward as that and together you may need to adapt the approach or use a combination of these introduced next.

Adapt the conflict mode

The TKI conflict mode instrument introduced in Chapter 2 is a valuable tool for reassessing the most beneficial resolution approach. Recognising your and the other person's default style in the conflict enables you to adapt your resolution style based on what's best for the situation. You may have started in competing mode seeking to get your way, but by reassessing, discovering compromising or collaborating is more effective. I had a client who had been avoiding addressing a direct report's underperformance. This manifested, leading her to deal with him in a raised voice using condescending remarks. One day he made another simple mistake that resulted in a financial loss and she immediately responded in a competing mode and implemented a performance improvement plan. He had also been avoiding the conflict, but when faced with being performance-managed, he also took to competing to defend his position by stating in writing that she was disrespectful to him. Communication had broken down between them and my client worked with me in coaching to find a constructive path forward. Objectively evaluating the situation by standing back from the situation, she aimed to change her communication approach, practising with me in various role-plays. She invited him to a meeting so they could work together on a mutually beneficial resolution. This approach encouraged him to shift away from a defensive stance and a competing approach. They both moved from a competing to a collaborative approach where they both got what they wanted – he would improve his accuracy and she would not shout at him.

Dialogue over debate

If both people are competing, the inclination is to engage in debate where each aims to convince the other that their perspective or agenda is correct. Debate assumes there's a right answer and can be useful when using facts or analysis to drive a decision. It can also involve scrutinising or cross-examining what the other person says or thinks. With debate, there's a risk of attacking the other person or their idea, and negative behaviours arise such as raised voices, interrupting, and being threatening or disrespectful. This results in toxic or unresolved conflict. The concept of dialogue is, as William Isaacs (2008) puts it is in his book title, The Art of Thinking Together. He explains the following behaviours essential to effective dialogue:

1. Listening. Creating space to listen rather than preparing to speak fosters understanding of each other's perspective. Recognising personal thoughts can interfere with what you think is happening, and can help you stick to the facts the other person says.
2. Respecting. Being respectful and accepting of the other's perspectives and boundaries enables further conversation. You don't have to think the same way, but notice the difference in opinions as an alternative way to see things. Isaacs calls this 'make it strange' (2008, p. 112). By seeing what is different, common ground can be found.
3. Suspending. When in conflict, it's easy to revert to thinking you know the right outcome. If you can leave that certainty until later, this provides space for more creative outcomes to materialise. Being aware and having the intention of waiting, prevents the pull to solve or fix disputes quickly at the risk of not fully exploring all options.

4. *Voicing.* Trusting your own voice, and being authentic in sharing your views and questioning others is important. But note that Isaacs states that learning to refrain from speaking in order to listen, and to consciously choose the words spoken rather than succumbing to pressure to speak, enables better ideas to unfold and be voiced as thoughts are given the space and time to be collected.

Transitioning conversations from debate to dialogue facilitates more creative solutions encouraging collaboration or compromise. Often, people are used to debate and it can be helpful if you introduce the concept of dialogue and suggest a shift to this approach. The key is to intentionally use dialogue to promote a different conversation. This may feel novel at first, and debate may re-emerge, so steering the conversation back to dialogue may be required.

Agenda setting or contracting

A constructive approach can include using agendas or contracting to establish how to work in healthy conflict. It clarifies expectations and establishes ground rules to help you both work through the conflict. Whether you need to introduce this approach to your counterpart, or you're a line manager or peer supporting others with conflict, you can guide the process. The approach can include a number of things relevant to your situation such as:

• Agreeing the ground rules for mutual respect, active listening, focusing on solving, ways of working, or introducing the concept of dialogue rather than debate, etc.
• Defining and agreeing on what the conflict is about.
• Identifying and prioritising goals or what the outcomes could be.
• Agreeing how to work together which may include responsibilities or who else needs to be involved.
• Setting milestones, timelines, and checkpoints.

This approach ensures a structured and transparent process to use together and can move conflict from unresolved or toxic and to healthy conflict.

Handle egos

Conflict can spiral when egos are involved, and it can be challenging to manage this. In competitive working environments, managing egos is essential for fostering healthy conflict and this will come down to a collective mindset where the issue at hand is deemed more important than an individual's own needs. Signs of ego involvement include defensiveness, resistance to feedback, blaming, finger-pointing, or being unwilling to compromise and sticking to the competitive mode. Ego can be related to yourself or the other person, as either or both of you can be at risk of behaving in this way. Being aware of your own ego and realising if you exhibit negative behaviours is important so you can check and manage yourself. To foster clear expectations of behaviour and a more professional working relationship, here are some strategies:

- Link to organisation or team values to highlight expectations aligned to culture.
- Establish clear mutual standards of working together linked to conduct, respect, collaboration, and trust.
- Encourage two-way feedback so both people's expectations can be regularly reviewed.
- Involve a third party such as leadership to help establish standards.

Set boundaries for yourself

Establishing boundaries can be useful, and requires commitment to assert them consistently to be effective. Melissa Urban (2022) looks at implementing boundaries for yourself and she says, 'Boundaries aren't about controlling the other person, they're about the limits you put in place around yourself to stay healthy and safe' (Urban, 2022, p. 36). She suggests there is no need to over-explain, justify or ask permission to set a boundary, but it is for the other person to respect it. Her approach includes setting a consequence to the boundary and enforcing it together with a traffic light approach. To illustrate how this works, here's an example of when one of my clients was struggling with his line manager who constantly criticised him in the open office. Often, his line manager would quickly forget about it when she'd had the chance to calm down. My client's boundary plan was as follows.

- Green – In a one-to-one meeting with his line manager he said 'When you criticise me in front of others, not only is it embarrassing for me, but others think it's unacceptable and have asked me if I am okay. If you have constructive feedback, please provide it in our one-to-one'.
- Yellow – If his line manager criticised him in the open office he planned to say 'Remember what I said, please be constructive and save it for our one-to-one'.
- Red – If his line manager continued to criticise, he would say 'It's not acceptable or appropriate to do this and I feel like you are bullying me. I will need to escalate this'.

He only had to implement the green boundary as his line manager was not aware of how she was coming across in the eyes of others or the impact it had on him, and immediately changed her behaviour. Implementing boundaries provides a practical way to manage what is acceptable for you and communicate these limits to others.

Engage support from others

There are occasions when the other person is uncooperative in resolving the issue or reluctant to take part in healthy conflict. They may have self-centred traits such as a lack of empathy or a tendency to manipulate and control, and dealing with these can be mentally draining and impact your wellbeing. Therefore, it's crucial to acknowledge this and seek support, especially in toxic conflict.

- **Authoritative person.** Consider escalating to a higher authority such as a line manager or project lead, particularly if there are time pressures or if attempts to manage the issue were unsuccessful. Be open to the other person and acknowledge that as you've both been unable to resolve or work through the conflict, that escalation is the next step. They may find it useful to escalate too. Escalation does not mean passing the responsibility on or complaining up the line, it's about trying to find a constructive way through the impasse.
- **Line manager.** Line managers, who you report to or have a dotted line into, can provide valuable insight and support due to their broader experience. They can provide a safe environment, remain neutral and

listen to help you assess what is happening. They may also be able to provide constructive feedback to assist in exploring alternative perspectives on how to address and resolve issues.

Summary

The process of dealing with two-party conflict may require multiple interventions with regular check-ins or follow-ups. Working through disagreements can be challenging, but leaving them ignored or not addressing the root cause could result in further tension, erosion of trust, missed opportunities for growth, and have an impact on mental health and wellbeing. Moreover, two-party conflict can negatively affect teams and work projects. While this chapter provides approaches that you can use by yourself to move to healthy conflict or resolution, there are times when support from an objective professional may be necessary, such as using a workplace mediator.

Key takeaways

- The intention to acknowledge and manage conflict is required otherwise conflict can repeat or become legacy conflict.
- When dealing with another person, taking an objective and non-personal perspective helps identify the stage and type of conflict experienced.
- Assessing an approach to adopt can be done individually, together or with another person.
- There are several approaches to choose from to move to healthy conflict and there will be occasions when you might choose more than one.

Reflective exercise

1. Think of a situation when you've had a conflict with another person and reflect on how you handled the situation.
2. Which approaches explored in this chapter could you have used to address the conflict with another person from question 1? What specifically might you have done?
3. What other key takeaways can you identify from this chapter?

References

Fisher, R, and Ury, W (1991). *Getting to Yes: Negotiating Agreement Without Giving In.* Penguin Books.

Gallo, A (2017). *HBR Guide to Dealing with Conflict (HBR Guide Series).* Harvard Business Review Press.

Goleman, D (1995). *Emotional Intelligence, Why It Can Matter More Than IQ.* Bloomsbury Publishing.

Harvard Business School (1979). Harvard negotiation project. Available at: https://www.pon.harvard.edu/category/research_projects/harvard-negotiation-project/ (accessed 18 December 2023).

Isaacs, W (2008). *Dialogue: The Art of Thinking Together.* The Crown Publishing Group.

Thomas, K W, and Kilmann, R H (1974). *Thomas-Kilmann Conflict Mode Instrument (TKI).* APA PsycTests. Available at: https://doi.org/10.1037/t02326-000 (accessed 16 October 2023).

Urban, M (2022). *The Book of Boundaries, Set the Limits That Will Set You Free.* Vermillion.

5

YOU AND OTHERS

Introduction

Dealing with conflict with yourself or another person can already be challenging, but when faced with more than one person, there can be a multitude of influences to make it even more difficult to deal with. Collaborating with multiple individuals is common and often essential at work. As the number of people you work with increases, this inevitably results in more chances of conflict arising. You could be leading a group of people or a team. You may also be part of a group or team without direct leadership responsibility. This chapter explores how and when conflict arises when working with more than one person, and introduces some additional approaches to use, building on previous chapters.

Exploring conflict with many others

When part of a group or team, it can be challenging to navigate differing interests, perspectives, objectives, and emotions. The terms groups and

DOI: 10.4324/9781041056461-7

teams are often used interchangeably because both are made up of a collection of individuals, however, there are slight nuances between them. A group has individuals with limited or no interdependency, where they may have their own or differing goals. A team is a form of a group, and Katzenbach and Smith's definition distinguishes what makes a group a genuine team:

> A team is a small number of people with complementary skills committed to a common purpose, performance goals and ways of working together for which they hold themselves mutually accountable.
>
> (1993, p. 69)

Whether working in formal groups such as a reporting team, or informal groups like at a conference or event, there is a consistent need to work with others, and the positive approaches in this chapter can help navigate conflict situations.

Recognising when there is conflict with others

When working in a group or team, the risk of conflict occurring will be high if the following has not been established: agreed goals, objectives, and priorities; and defined roles and responsibilities. Furthermore, mutual trust, respect and open communication can prevent toxic or unresolved conflict (conflict triangle). However, even with this, disagreements can occur. Recognising the conflict stage helps to understand when and how to approach it. Bruce Tuckman's Team Development model (1965) provides a guide to help with this and has five stages.

1. **Forming** is when individuals come together where there may be a lack of formal structure. Examples could be when there is a business issue requiring a quick resolution such as a sprint that pulls experts together from different areas. This can be the pre-conflict stage as people start to get to know each other. Early indications of personalities, goals, objectives and priorities may start to arise and there may be unresolved conflict as people may be more polite, uncertain of what's required, and may ignore or wait to avoid raising any controversy.
2. **Storming** occurs as individuals start to organise themselves and tensions might arise as goals or expectations are established, or there may be clashes over power, roles and responsibilities. In the previous

example of a sprint, people start to realise the amount of work involved or have different opinions on what needs to be done. Often this will be the during conflict stage with the risk of toxic conflict occurring if clarity and agreement on a way forward is not mutually established.

3. **Norming** is when trust starts developing, interpersonal relationships grow and there is focus on aligning goals or objectives. There can be healthy conflict during this stage if there is psychological safety for people to contribute, express ideas and share problem-solving ideas together. An example could be a board leadership team sharing information and ideas, working together to create strategy and taking shared responsibility.

4. **Performing** is where individuals work optimally together, understand each other, and have interdependence when individuals can work on their own, in a smaller sub-group or part of the whole unit. An example could be a business unit team that has worked together for a while, where individuals work together like a well-oiled machine. Not all groups or teams reach this stage. Healthy conflict is common during the performing stage as collaboration, creativity and clear objectives provide clarity on what is required.

5. **Adjourning** occurs when the group or team disbands, for example, a project team that has completed launching a product. There may be an unresolved conflict here as issues may have been parked or not prioritised to protect the project delivery. There can often be a lack of time to tie up loose ends or review lessons learned as individuals move on to different work.

When working with others, reflecting on the development stage of the group or team can provide insight into when conflict may occur and the

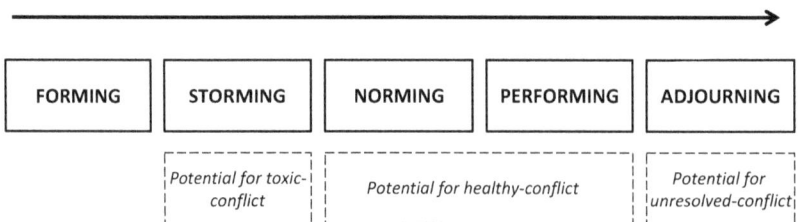

Figure 5.1 Example of conflict during team development stages, adapted from Tuckman (1965)

risk of the conflict. However, it's not always clear-cut because any type of conflict can occur when working with others, and there is potential for conflict to occur concurrently with different types of disagreements.

How conflict with others can occur

As people work together, conflict can occur in various ways which depend on a number of factors. While working with my clients on conflict, here are some of the more common fundamental reasons which influence the rise of disagreements at work and some ideas on what can be done to address them.

Different personality traits and preferences

In research by the Chartered Institute of Personnel and Development (CIPD) almost half of employees surveyed stated differences in personality styles of working as a factor that drove the conflict. Furthermore, respect was highlighted as a key driving behaviour and the report stated, 'This finding underlies the importance of healthy and respectful relationships, and how commonly their absence can trigger conflict between people' (Stuff, 2020, p. 17). Individuals have different approaches to work and their behaviours can be driven by their personality profiles which can cause potential stress points when working together.

As explored in Chapter 3, when looking at understanding your behaviours, tools such as personality profiling can also be used with groups or teams to help understand and work better with each other. Undertaking personality profiling together provides useful insight which enables you to adapt your approach when relevant. A team-building activity specifically incorporating results of profiling and applying them to a work disagreement can provide a live example for everyone to work with. If it's not possible to undertake formal profiling, an informal approach can be as effective and can be done through observing and noting what others' behaviours, preference styles to work or communication styles are. A more qualitative approach such as a session with open conversation for everyone to share their preferences, strengths, etc can generate insights into how people can work together effectively.

Weak interpersonal stakeholder relationships

Groups or teams are made up of relationships, and as Humprey et al. stated, '… more than a specific collection of members, it is the collection of dyadic relationships or interactions between members that brings teams into existence' (2017, p. 59). Strong professional relationships with trust and respect are crucial for healthy conflict that enables collaboration, contributing to better productivity and innovation. The way in which relationships can be built and maintained was explored in Chapter 2, and the stakeholder plan (Table 2.1) is a key tool to use when working with others. You may find groups of individuals can be managed together such as those with similar objectives, interests or perspectives. This can be replicated onto a stakeholder plan to enable you to work with groups within the wider group or team. Ways to improve relationships can be done by building trust through how you communicate with them, being empathetic about their needs and valuing their perspectives, demonstrating your competence or expertise and fulfilling any commitments to build your credibility.

Strong stakeholder relationships are key in dealing with conflict as these people can become advocates of you and what you are doing. It can be a struggle to influence people with your ideas or proposals during a meeting when time is limited or if they have not had time to reflect on what you share. To prevent it from leading to toxic conflict and to maintain healthy conflict, preparing stakeholders beforehand is crucial. A topic clients often bring to coaching is how to prevent conflict during decision-making meetings. It's common to prefer no questions or disagreements when presenting a proposal and tempting to want to bring a well-prepared proposal to a decision-making meeting such as a steering committee in the hope it gets agreed. However, the slick PowerPoint presentation usually provides new information, data and ideas, which others may be unfamiliar with and before you know it, a barrage of challenges, questions, and disagreement occurs. Encouraging healthy conflict will make it easier to manage and result in better outcomes. Meetings can be a place for decisions to be discussed, however, there is often limited time to fully explore or discuss information and time pressures can result in stakeholders feeling uncertain or anxious and they may behave defensively, resistant or question the proposal. To avoid this, it can be helpful to prepare stakeholders in advance, rather than surprising them with your new proposal. This can be done by:

- Engaging with them during the ideation or development of your proposal to ensure they are aware of the potential changes or topics.
- Meeting with them individually to discuss the impact on their area to gauge their opinions and sentiment, and so that you can address them accordingly.
- Providing the presentation in advance, enabling them to send questions to you before the meeting so you can answer them directly beforehand, or prepare to acknowledge and address them during the meeting.

This approach is not about preventing conflict, it is about addressing disagreements upfront and paving the way for healthy conflict. If there is still disagreement that arises during the meeting, it's likely that healthy conflict will enable a culture of being open and collaborative to address unforeseen or unintended consequences of the proposal.

Lack of cultural awareness

At work, there are rich opportunities to engage with individuals from different cultures derived from different countries. The various perspectives that stem from working in different countries provide experiences and norms that can challenge groups or teams working together. Conflict can arise from stereotyping and invisible boundaries such as the unspoken or subtle cultural norms people live by. This can result in misinterpretations or misunderstandings. Being open to difference is not enough to be able to leverage and embrace the diversity; truly understanding differences and adapting your approach can help to minimise or address conflict. Erin Meyer's (2014) research demonstrates how people from different countries behave across eight dimensions which is highlighted in Table 5.1 with a simple question to help you understand each dimension.

It's important to note two things when using this approach. The first is that although individuals from specific countries may appear positioned at various points on a scale, these positions are not fixed. Instead, they are relative positions to people from the other countries and their positions on the scale. The other is that the placement of people from each country is not always the rule and that this research provides trends as a guide to help us understand how to work with others from different cultures.

Table 5.1 Eight dimensions to consider when working across cultures, based on Meyer (2002)

Communicating	Are they low-context communicating in simple, verbose, and clear terms, or high-context where there is rich and deep meaning in interactions?
Evaluating	When giving negative feedback is it given directly, or is the preference to be indirect and discreet?
Persuading	Do they like to hear specific cases and examples, or prefer holistic explanations?
Leading	Are people in groups egalitarian, or do they prefer hierarchy?
Deciding	Are decisions made in consensus, or made with a top-down approach?
Trusting	Do people base trust on how well they perform tasks, or on a relationship approach?
Disagreeing	Are disagreements tackled directly, or do people prefer to avoid discussing them?
Scheduling	Do they perceive time as absolute linear points, or consider it as a flexible range?

For example, from the research, Germans were found to give more direct negative feedback in relation to the French, but this does not mean that every German behaves this way. Or where people from China have a more hierarchical approach than those from Japan who are more consensual driven; however, again, there will be times when individuals don't behave this way, especially when there may be team or organisational culture factors at play. An individual's own personal values and perspectives may also drive different behaviours. Furthermore, how they behave might be influenced by the industry they work in, their profession or job role, and the organisation, which is explored in the next chapter.

It should also be noted that with migration trends, there are additional factors to consider such as where individuals were born and brought up, or perhaps they have worked in several different countries which adds to their cultural diversity. These individuals are known to be more adept at adapting their approaches, as Pollock et al. (2017) discuss and there may be 'hidden diversity' (2017, p. 418), where differences are not apparent. Being mindful of this reduces the risk of conflict from cultural stereotyping or assumptions. It is helpful to appreciate and recognise there could be differences in how individuals think, perceive things and behave, due to the cultural influences in their backgrounds. If in doubt, open and sensitive communication with others can help distil any uncertainty and be more aware of differences. This increased awareness can help you adjust your approach in response to this.

Misaligned goals, objectives, or priorities

Diverging or different perspectives can stem from different goals, objectives, or priorities individuals have when working together. Thus, a fundamental part of working in groups or teams is to have clear goals or objectives of why the group or team is working together. This will set the boundaries and guidelines for how to work together. For example, when working on a sprint project, individuals from different business areas are put together to solve a problem or deliver something within a short timeframe. They will have different reasons for being allocated to the project, such as to gain visibility, to engage in stretch work experience, to solve the problem, to ensure compliance with regulations, commercial viability, or customer centricity, etc. Thus, these different objectives can cause friction when working intensely together with short timescales. There will also be an overarching and overall project goal, which everyone needs to be aware of and focused on. There might be a document that outlines this, or in some cases, an email providing limited details. People may have received different levels of information about the project. Therefore, an open conversation to clarify, agree and document the goal is not only useful for the project but important to minimise conflict when disagreements occur. During this process, the opportunity for each individual to share their own goals or objectives is also useful. When conflict arises, reminding everyone of the agreed goal helps refocus on what is important. If the scope or objectives change as the project progresses, a revisit of the initial agreed goal may be required to see what needs to be adapted. Throughout the project, there may also be the need for individuals to reassess their own goals to determine if they are in line with what the group is working on.

Unclear roles and responsibilities

There are several ways in which the different roles and responsibilities of individuals working together can produce conflict. When there is ambiguity in terms of unclear or overlapping roles, this can result in conflict over who is accountable or makes decisions. When there is a clear hierarchy in the form of a clear leader, or perhaps an imbalance of power, this can also produce conflict when people disagree with each other. When working across functions, this often occurs due to different expectations, goals or approaches when working together. Clarification of the clear roles and responsibilities will support how decisions are made, and how to make best use of each other's strengths or experience, to increase collaborative working to be more effective.

Dysfunctional teams

Have you ever found yourself in a situation where the team you are in has an inability to work cohesively together? Or perhaps interpersonal issues or styles of communication prevent effective work outputs? A dysfunctional team is often one where power struggles, competitive behaviours, and toxic conflict occur. Lencioni (2002) states if there is no trust, little ability to resolve conflict, no commitment as a team, little accountability, and a lack of results-focus, then the team will be dysfunctional. Leaders of teams can think about developing a team through the five stages in Figure 5.2. Lencioni sees this as a sequence of five stages where each stage must be achieved before the next in order to have the foundations for building a

Take each stage
at a time as each
is required
before the next

5. TOGETHER FOCUS ON RESULTS

4. HAVE ACCOUNTABILITY

3. COMMIT TO EACH OTHER AND TEAM

2. HAVE HEALTHY-CONFLICT

1. BUILD TRUST

Figure 5.2 Based on Five dysfunctions of a team, Lencioni (2002)

functional team. First, there must be trust with open and honest communication in a psychologically safe environment where opinions and ideas can be expressed without fear. This paves the way for healthy conflict where differing viewpoints can be worked through. With that there must be a commitment to support each other from everyone and in doing so, clear alignment of goals and objectives. Then each member must be committed and accountable individually and as a group or team, and hold each other accountable to promote a mutually responsible culture. Finally, if they can focus on achieving results as a collective, rather than just focusing on their own individual results, this collaborative approach can enable success for them all.

Practical positive approaches to get to healthy conflict

STOP!

Similar to dealing with conflict within yourself or with another person, the important thing to remember is to acknowledge what is happening. Take a pause to reflect and have the intention to do something about what is happening. Whether you are involved with the conflict, or you see it happening with the people you are working with, you can support the situation by taking this step. It may be an opportune time to reflect on whether you seem to be on your own in your opinions versus what others think, or perhaps you may identify others who have similar opinions or goals to you. If the situation is that you are an outlier, it's useful to remain open-minded to avoid the risk of reacting emotionally or defensively and to try not to take it personally.

Choose your role

Depending on the situation, it's important to decide on what role you want to take in the conflict. Being a facilitator and taking the lead to support the group or team to work through disagreements is an option where you maintain control of the process and ensure a balanced or rounded outcome is achieved. Zubizarreta (2015) talks about moving conflict to creative collaboration using dynamic facilitation (Rough, 1997), which uses exploration as a means to work collaboratively and creatively, to solve problems and in decision-making. Dynamic facilitation is non-linear and enables discussions to flow naturally by encouraging different aspects of the issue to arise. This can take some time, but ensuring there is the space to explore, allows everyone's skills, knowledge and experience to be harnessed. This leads to creative thinking and better innovative solutions. When using this approach, your role moves to a neutral one where you focus on directing the process, and should not steer the content of the discussion nor direct the outcome.

If you feel you have a stake in what or how the conflict is resolved and want to ensure your voice is considered amongst everyone else's, consider how you can position yourself as part of the process. Introducing the dialogue approach covered in the previous chapter can put some structure around the communication approach. There may be times for the need to take a facilitative role to marshal or remind everyone of how you've all agreed to work together. However, this can be challenging to do if you wish to be a key contributor to the discussion. In these circumstances it may be prudent to seek someone else to facilitate the process, such as a colleague who does not have an interest in the work or an independent external facilitator.

The Thomas–Kilmann Conflict Model, introduced in Chapter 2, are valuable to refer to when working in groups. There may be occasions when it may be beneficial to adopt a more passive role in the avoiding mode, if the issue isn't something that impacts you or your own team or where you hold no direct responsibility over. Or perhaps the conflict regards something you have little or no interest in and you might choose to accommodate others as the impact on you is low, or you may wish to save your effort for another conflict which is more significant to you or where you are more invested in the outcome.

However, for leaders or those who want to take the lead, it might become a duty to acknowledge and support others in dealing with the conflict. 'To approach conflict as a coaching leader, you choose courage to acknowledge and call it out' (Kim, 2020, p. 31). In doing so, you encourage conflicts to be addressed constructively which paves the way for healthy conflict. As a group, the collaborating or compromising modes are particularly useful when working together as this allows diverse perspectives to be harnessed to address challenges together for better overall outcomes.

Contracts or agreements

When working on formal projects, there is often a project charter that keeps all stakeholders aligned to the purpose of the work, vision, goals, roles and responsibilities, timescales, budgets, and other relevant details required for the particular project. It is an important document as it ensures all stakeholders have a shared and agreed understanding of how they will reach the outcome required. This formality kicks off projects and can be revisited when issues or disagreements arise. There may be times when there has not been genuine commitment from everyone or as the project progresses it is evident that what's in the document is not lived and breathed when working together. Referring everyone back to this document during these occasions can be a helpful reminder.

However, sometimes formalities of a contract or agreement are not in place. This could be when in a functional team or working in groups or teams on activities not set up as formal projects. Ideally, setting up a contract or agreement during the pre-conflict stage can set the sentiment for healthy conflict when disagreements arise. But there is also a benefit in setting this up later when in the during conflict stage too. The contract or agreement need not be as formal as a project charter but may include similar information as depicted in but not limited to Figure 5.3. A contract or agreement to ways of working can include whatever your group decides is useful. Some examples could be: the roles and responsibilities of each individual and their objectives; which modes of communication are used and how often they are used for business-as-usual issues and for extraordinary, urgent, or unforeseen issues; how people treat each other, which may include specific points such as with respect, share of voice, no interruptions, etc.; how decisions are made, particularly when disagreements arise and this could include voting systems, escalation points, open discussion, etc.

Contract or agreement

1. Goals, objectives and priorities
2. Roles and responsibilities
3. Methods of communication
4. Decision-making methods
5. Treatment of each other

Figure 5.3 Example of what to put in a group or team contract or agreement

CASE STUDY G

Ushi and team disagreements

Ushi worked within a team which she likened to being in a family. The way they treated each other had become over-familiar and disagreements often occurred in the open plan office for all to witness. They truly believed that what they had was an open and honest approach to handling disagreements, and although there was a sense of camaraderie due to the high levels of trust between them, often emotions would run high with raised voices and inappropriate language for the work environment.

It took someone on another team to point out how uncomfortable it made others feel and how disruptive it was to other colleagues when disagreements occurred. Ushi was surprised and embarrassed that others perceived them in this way. She highlighted this to her team and that the unintended consequences of what they thought was healthy conflict were seen as toxic conflict and disruptive to others. The team were so entrenched in their ways of working that they had not realised this. This resulted in them revisiting the way they communicated with each other and agreed an informal contract which included tone of voice, respect, a level of professionalism, listening to each other without interruption and taking disagreements into a private room when necessary.

The key is for everyone to contribute and agree to what is in the contract or agreement that becomes a working document which is revisited and revised at key points such as when disagreements occur or when individuals stray from what was agreed. There is value in doing this at any time, such as in the during conflict stage or when in toxic conflict. Having agreed ways of working paves the way for healthy conflict.

Open communication, feedback, and reflection

Having open communication, feedback and reflection are practical approaches to use in daily working life and crucial for encouraging healthy conflict. Open communication involves everyone feeling there is psychological safety to have a transparent and honest exchange of opinions, information and ideas. Being able to feedback with constructive and specific examples or information regarding behaviours, actions or ideas, in a timely manner, helps keep channels of communication open. Then using feed-back to reflect on the conflict dynamics can help identify potential triggers, themes of people's emotions or perspectives, etc. which can drive the right approaches to use to manage or resolve disagreement. However, it's all too easy to omit one or all three of these areas when faced with the challenges of a fast-paced work environment. When it comes to conflict, these three things – that is, open communication, feedback and reflection, are par-ticularly beneficial, especially when working with many other individuals.

CASE STUDY H

Salma and her team

Salma was brought in as an experienced Head of Operations to improve efficiency for the team of fifty with three sub-teams. After six months, she had their first staff survey and the results were poor. The survey highlighted low morale, leadership and collaboration scores, with a high percentage of staff looking to leave. She felt frustrated, angry and inse-cure with the constant conflict she was experiencing with the team in the form of pushback, disagreements, and at worse being ignored. She explored what had happened in the first few months and realised she had restructured the team, overhauled and introduced new processes, and implemented her changes. Upon further reflection she realised that in her attempt to demonstrate strong leadership, she had done it all with-out input or dialogue with her team. The impact on the team was confu-sion and annoyance. The changes meant they had adapted or changed responsibilities, and resulted in a decrease in productivity as they strug-gled with the new processes. Furthermore, a breakdown in communica-tion was evident because any challenges or opinions they voiced were not taken on board by Salma.

As she reflected on this, she realised her top-down approach had not included any of her team in the decision-making of the changes and she purely expected them to implement them. The clarity and focus she thought they needed may have been taken as somewhat dictatorial.

To address the conflict she identified three priority areas to work on.

1. Engaging her team. She developed a stakeholder plan which ena-bled her to realise the importance of adopting a collaborative approach with her three direct reports. When she opened up the

communication with them, this resulted in her learning they had more expertise in their areas than she did and as they preferred and were used to working with autonomy, they wanted to support the changes by reviewing the new processes to adapt them appropriately.

2. Gaining buy-in for the changes from her team. She invited her team to use open dialogue during team meetings to discuss the changes and the rationale behind them and provided opportunity for them to voice concerns and provide constructive suggestions for them to consider and work through together to resolve.

3. Building team morale. She took advice and was guided by her direct reports on what could help build morale, and they suggested having a whole team meeting focused on rebuilding trust and morale.

These were just the start of her commitments to dealing with the conflict, and it paved the way to a more collaborative approach where there was psychological safety for the team to work up and down the hierarchy to review and implement the appropriate changes to drive the efficiencies required.

Group think

A strong group identity can be powerful when working on a common agenda or goal. However, there is a risk that group think occurs where individuals tend to accept or conform to the same viewpoint. 'One of the main characteristics of group think is that, in an effort to demonstrate harmony and unity, people fail to consider alternative perspectives and ultimately engage in deeply problematic decision-making' (Allen and Howell, 2020, p. 16). Allen and Howell warn that with group think and addressing conflict, there is the risk of limited critical evaluation or discussion of problems or disagreements that may arise. This may cause the group to avoid dealing with disagreement resulting in unresolved conflict, as there may be pressure to conform.

Sometimes, there may be a strong sub-group which clings together that is hard to persuade such as a commercial team who purely wants to focus and make decisions based on financial returns when discussing a new customer proposal. An approach to use could be to break the group up and work with them individually to understand their perspectives and concerns. In doing so, there may be one or more of the group who have an alternative way of thinking and feel the same as you and be a potential advocate. Having individual conversations can provide insight into what concerns the group has and potential advocates can support a more open discussion to any disagreements as they have your support too. It's also easier to influence individuals who may then be able to follow through with the rest of their sub-group.

Another method to combat group think is breaking the group or team into smaller groups. This has been an effective in-person approach if there is space within or outside the main room, and more commonly adopted since the increased move to virtual working. This enables two levels of participation, one with everyone together and the other in smaller groups (Danskin and Lind, 2014, p. 80). Using small breakout groups with a minimum of two people in each encourages more communication and participation so different viewpoints can arise and be worked on in the smaller group. The disagreement could be broken up so each breakout group has an element of the disagreement to work through, or they could all work on the whole disagreement. Sharing ideas back together can surface the key themes and identify new thinking to work through conflict, while providing everyone with the chance to input.

Lack of alliances

When in groups or teams, it can be useful to identify who your allies are. Allies in the workplace are those who share interests or can merge efforts for mutual benefit. Allies can be temporary, such as when working on a work activity or project who have similar perspectives and ideas as you do, and where you support each other. Allies can also be more long-standing when colleagues support each other due to the strong relationships formed from previous experiences working together such as colleagues who started in the organisation together and went through the same training programme. When there is the potential for conflict or when in the thick of disagreement or misunderstandings, alliances can support each other in aligning efforts or ideas which can be further supported by coordinating actions or strategies. There may also be allies outside of the group or team who can help influence or support you during conflict. The Power–Interest Matrix covered in Chapter 2 can help you identify who these stakeholders are.

When to escalate

As conflict is a common occurrence when working with many people, it's usual for the group or team to attempt to resolve the conflict or get to a healthy conflict themselves first. However, there may be times when it's prudent to refer to someone else such as a line manager or accountable executive, such as when there is a risk to timelines, quality of the work or impacts to resources. There might be occasions to escalate to organisational process owners such as legal, compliance or human resources teams. These could be where there are potential regulatory breaches or ethically driven conflicts that might include bullying or harassment. For occasions such as these, engaging an impartial and experienced mediator can also be an effective option to consider and this is explored in Chapter 9.

Summary

It is inevitable that when working with other people there will be the risk of disagreements arising. The more you collaborate with others, and the more you experience interacting with different people, the higher the chances of conflict. Understanding each others' perspectives, goals, roles, and responsibilities can help you manage the situation through effective stakeholder engagement.

Key takeaways

- There are various scenarios at work when conflict can arise when engaging with multiple individuals which may be in a group or team setting. These are complex and may require a combination of different approaches to be adopted.
- As a group or team develops, recognising the conflict stage can help you understand the chances of disagreement arising and be prepared for it with approaches to use to encourage healthy conflict.
- When working with more than one person, awareness of personality traits, strong interpersonal relationships, cultural awareness, aligned goals, and clear roles and responsibilities can foster open communication by laying the foundations in the form of contracts or agreements for ways of working.

- Group think is a risk that can be counter-balanced with smaller group work that helps to address and navigate conflict while engaging and encouraging participation, and can produce more innovative or creative solutions.

Reflective exercise

1. Identify a current or previous situation when you have experienced conflict within a group or team.
2. What factors led to the conflict?
3. Which approaches explored in this chapter could have been useful to manage the group or team during that conflict?
4. Which approach do you think may not work and why would this be?
5. What is something new you have taken away from this chapter?

References

Allen, DM, and Howell, JW (2020). *Groupthink in Science – Greed, Pathological Altruism, Ideology, Competition and Culture*. Springer.

Danskin, K, and Lind, L (2014). *Virtuous Meetings: Technology and Design For High Engagement In Large Groups*. Jossey-Bass.

Humphrey, SE, Aime, F, Cushenbery, L, Hill, AD, and Fairchild, J (September 2017). Team conflict dynamics: Implications of a dyadic view of conflict for team performance. *Organizational Behavior and Human Decision Processes*, Vol. 142, pp. 58–70.

Katzenbach, JR, and Smith, DK (1993). The wisdom of teams. *Small Business Reports*, Vol 18, No 7, p. 68.

Kim, H (2020). *Soft Skills For Hard People – A Practical Guide to Emotional Intelligence For Rational Leaders*. Paper Raven Books.

Lencioni, P (2002). *The Five Dysfunctions of a Team: A Leadership Fable*. Jossey-Bass.

Meyer, E (2014). *The Culture Map – Decoding How People Think, Lead, and Get Things Done Across Cultures*. Public Affairs.

Pollock, DC, Van Reken, RE, and Pollock, MV (2017). *Third Culture Kids*. Nicholas Brealey Publishing.

Rough, J (1997). Dynamic facilitation and the magic of self-organizing change. *The Journal for Quality and Participation*, Vol. 20, Issue 3, pp. 34–38.

Stuff, R (2020). *Managing Conflict in the Workplace*. Chartered Institute of Personnel and Development.

Tuckman, BW (1965). Developmental sequence in small groups. *Psychological Bulletin*, Vol 63, pp. 384–399.

Zubizarreta, R (2015). *From Conflict To Creative Collaboration*. Two Harbors Press.

6

ORGANISATIONAL CONFLICT

Introduction

The term organisational conflict commonly refers to any conflict occurring in the workplace or conflict between co-workers. Here, we look at the conflict that arises from systemic drivers within organisations, such as organisational culture or styles of leadership. These may be so deeply ingrained and interwoven into the nature of the organisation, that any arising conflict may seem or may even be outside of what you think you may be able to influence. This chapter continues to build on previous chapters and introduces some approaches that can be adopted to manage conflict or encourage healthy conflict.

Understanding organisations

A little understanding of organisational behaviour can provide insight into workplace culture. Davis (1968) illustrated four behavioural styles that can influence the type of culture that occurs within organisations.

DOI: 10.4324/9781041056461-8

1. **Autocratic** relates to power where the leadership is more formal and official, similar to a command approach.
2. **Custodial** is where leaders are seen as caring and focused on fostering employee loyalty, often through perks or benefits such as incentives or healthcare.
3. **Supportive** seeks to understand employee motivations and provides support to inspire them to develop and succeed.
4. **Collegial** focuses on developing a degree of shared power, where leaders coach and employees feel invested in the organisation's success.

Organisations may lean towards one approach or have a combination of more than one. Sub-groups may exhibit one approach over another, influenced by leaders' preferences within those groups. Conflict may occur in all four cultures and can have an impact on morale and overall performance depending on how it is managed. Furthermore, with certain cultures, such as autocratic ones, the risk of unresolved conflict can be high as employees might not be able to challenge or address disagreements themselves because the leadership determines the direction. Awareness of your own particular leadership approach (autocratic, custodial, supportive, or collegial) in relation to the organisation's cultural leadership approach provides insight into how and when conflict arises and impacts you or your colleagues. Adapting or flexing between the leadership approaches can be effective in different scenarios such as using a supportive approach with your team when the overall organisation may be more autocratic, or providing a more autocratic approach when there is a need for it such as in an emergency.

Organisational lifecycles

Organisations have a lifecycle with theory stemming back to the 1930s (Mooney and Reiley, 1931). Common themes are seen across various models and can be applied to different types of organisations, from sole proprietorships to multi-national corporations. The following stages typically encapsulate stages of an organisation's lifecycle.

1. **Seed and development** is when a new business idea is conceptualised and funding might be sought.

2. **Launch or startup** is when the business is founded and the focus is on developing products or services to enter the marketplace.
3. **Growth** is when there is expansion of revenue, customers and market share with the focus shifting to scaling.
4. **Maturity** is the period when growth levels off and the focus might be on maximising profitability, optimising operations or keeping market share.
5. **Renewal and reinvention** is when organisations explore how to adapt to the changing market, regain, or grow competitiveness through innovation, such as rebranding or developing new products or services.
6. **Decline** is when there may be declining commercials such as income or sales, changes to the market due to customer preferences, technological changes, competitors, or regulation. This could result in cost-cutting or restructuring activity.
7. **Exit or transformation** is when the company may dissolve, be acquired, or merged, or undergoes significant transformation such as restructuring, diversification into new markets or ownership changes.

Figure 6.1 demonstrates a linear path, but organisations can repeat or omit stages e.g. at transformation they can go back to growth, maturity, and renewal or reinvention, or go from growth to exit immediately if the business is not viable.

Disagreements can occur as a result of the stage the organisation is at and being aware of the stage can provide insight into why or how it can arise which can help navigate how it is managed. For example, during the growth stage, rapid expansion may arise and as the structure evolves, there might be challenges on how processes or systems should develop. In the maturity stage or renewal or reinvention stage, there may be some

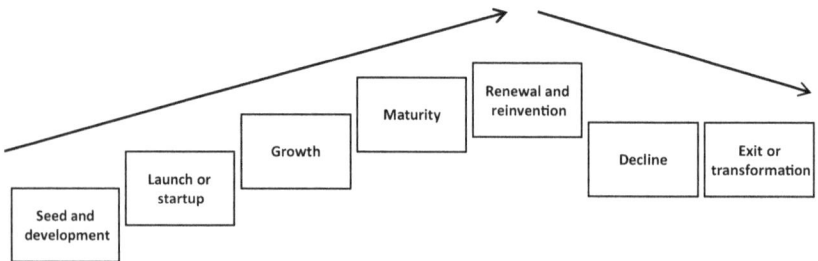

Figure 6.1 Typical stages of organisation lifecycles

resistance to adopting a more innovative approach or to which direction the organisation should take, causing conflict for those involved. In the decline stage or transformation stage, financial pressures or external threats can result in diverging interests or priorities for stakeholders associated with how to manage the organisation. Thus recognising the stage of the organisation's life cycle provides an understanding of any disagreements or challenges at each stage.

CASE STUDY I

Alexis in a startup

Alexis's goal was to support a small technology business looking to scale. Her background was risk and a business with an exciting vision welcomed her as a Non-Executive Director. During her first 100 days in the role, she started to experience conflict. The business focused on rapid product innovation over risk management and financial planning, favouring short-term gains over long-term sustainability. This concerned Alexis as she naturally had a risk-averse approach. She often highlighted the importance of mitigating risks she could foresee which led to tensions during board meetings and the founders regarded her as overly cautious and resistant to change.

She competed to have her opinions considered and questioned her ability to support them. Whilst researching and reflecting on this, she realised these were common startup situations and focused on how to adapt her approach to better handle the conflict that arose. She began introducing a dialogue approach to encourage healthy-conflict discussions rather than a debate-style conversation which enabled the board to have a more collaborative conversation. She also leveraged Thomas–Kilmann Conflict Mode Instrument (TKI; Thomas and Kilmann, 1974) introduced in Chapter 2, which provided her with a practical way to navigate different circumstances.

How organisational conflict can occur

There are a multitude of reasons why organisational conflict occurs including factors such as resource constraints, changes to strategic direction or priorities, leadership or management styles, breakdown in communication, stakeholder interests, or external influences, such as regulation, competition, or market access.

Lack of clear vision or strategy

A lack of a clear vision or strategy or the process of developing a clear vision and strategy can bring disagreements as key parties may or may not agree with it. When involved in this, each stakeholder has vested interests in what this can look like, based on their department or own opinions. If the vision or strategy is not clearly articulated to the rest of the organisation, this can produce uncertainty or confusion as employees struggle to align their work priorities, be inconsistent in decision-making or hinder accountability. Communication risks being inconsistent with mixed or incoherent messages causing mistrust or loss in confidence as employees don't understand or see why things are done. Furthermore, resources or effort may be wasted as a result of inefficiencies or missed opportunities.

Changing goals, objectives, or priorities

When there is a lack of clear vision or strategy, there is a risk of changing or different goals, objectives, or priorities. There is potential for disagreements or wrong decisions to be made as stakeholders have diverging ideas on how to address challenges or opportunities. In business environments a constant flux of change is common which can impact goals, objectives, and priorities. The United States Army War College (1987) popularised Bennis and Nanus' (1986) work with the concept of a VUCA environment, which they explain as:

- **Volatility,** where there is rapid and unpredictable change.
- **Uncertainty,** where there is a lack of clarity on what is currently happening or what may happen in the future.
- **Complexity,** with various influencing factors driving the potential for confusion, misunderstanding, and chaos.
- **Ambiguity,** where there is a lack of clarity or awareness of what the situation is.

This term is widely used in the business world as organisations constantly work in a VUCA environment. Within organisations, people may be resistant to or uncomfortable working with the unpredictability of a VUCA world and thus this can give rise to conflict.

Dysfunctional or clashing teams or business units

In organisations dysfunctional teams may emerge with ineffective leadership, lack of focus, accountability or avoidance of responsibility. This can result in people operating in an environment that lacks trust and where there is poor communication. When faced with working within these areas it can take a toll on wellbeing and mental health.

Interdepartmental or business unit clashes might arise when there are conflicting goals or priorities, resource constraints, power struggles or interdepartmental rivalries. This becomes particularly evident in matrix organisations where two or more types of organisational structures are combined such as functional, e.g. finance, compliance, marketing, etc., and projects, e.g. product lines or services. This convergence can result in overlapping and multiple reporting lines. According to Barker et al. (1988, p. 167), conflicts in matrix organisations can happen due to adopting competitive and avoiding modes of the TKI model. Although matrix structuring can improve collaboration, break down silos and increase efficiencies, conflict can occur due to divided loyalties, blurred accountability or power struggles. Thus, effectively managing this requires open communication, clarification of roles and responsibilities to foster trust, collaboration, and shared accountability.

Lack of congruence

When there is a mismatch between individuals and the organisation in terms of values, beliefs, work styles, or communication approaches, individuals may find the organisation challenging to work in. Typical examples could include:

- Mismatch of job roles where there is a disconnect in what the job description states to the job in practice or a difference in expectations of what the individual thought was required.

- Lack of recognition leading to employees feeling undervalued or unappreciated.
- Work–life balance where conflict arises when individuals are unable to balance their work and personal responsibilities.
- Ethical issues such as if an employee is asked to do something that is against their personal or professional ethics.
- Management styles or leadership approaches that an employee does not agree with.
- Violation of rights may occur due to breaches of contracts or unfair dismissal.
- Cultural fit where an individual does not fit into the organisation's culture which may impact their ability to perform or progress in the organisation.
- Values clash where an individual's values do not match the organisation's values or ways of doing things.

This can lead to frustration or disengagement especially if the individual has tried to challenge ways of working, attempted to adapt to the organisation or tries to ignore the misalignment.

On the other hand, a lack of congruence might be beneficial for organisations as individuals can challenge norms to come up with better or alternative approaches. There are times when people are recruited specifically to do this to add to the culture, and this improves diversity of thinking and working. In a Forbes article, Snow (2020) said,

> We worry that different personalities and perspectives and ways of approaching things will create conflict, so much that even when we do staff up with different kinds of people, we have a tendency to fear the friction that results. But that cognitive friction turns out to be the very thing that helps groups of disparate people become more than the sum of their parts!
>
> (Snow, 2020)

For individuals who are hired on this basis, the tendency to experience conflict is high and having this awareness beforehand and when they are in the organisation is crucial so they can adopt positive approaches to handle these situations and protect their mental health and wellbeing.

Practical positive approaches to get to healthy conflict

Navigating conflict can be challenging especially when the influencing factors seem or feel beyond your control. However, there are some practical and positive approaches worth considering. The success of each approach is dependent on the situation, but clients often are surprised at how they can make a positive impact which supports their and others' overall mental health and wellbeing.

Create psychological safety

The fear of speaking up or openly disagreeing can have negative consequences on mental health and wellbeing resulting in unresolved conflict. Contrastingly, if there is a culture of being able to say whatever people think, without fear or repercussions, this can lead to toxic conflict. Psychological safety is where speaking up, taking risks and being your authentic self is respected. It creates an environment where constructive communication can take place in a professional manner. Clark (2020) explains that with both permission and respect, there are four stages of psychological safety.

1. **Inclusion safety** is where there is belonging and acceptance, regardless of differences and where diversity is respected.
2. **Learner safety** is where there is the ability to learn, develop and discover through asking questions, giving and receiving feedback, experimenting, and the chance to make mistakes.
3. **Contributor safety** is where meaningful contributions are welcomed based on skills, knowledge, and experience.
4. **Challenger safety** allows the challenging of the status quo or addressing disagreements without risk of it impacting you or the fear of reprisal.

Figure 6.2 shows how this enables employees to engage in healthy conflict against the level of safety they may feel when faced with navigating disagreements. Feeling included will help build confidence to enable a learning environment. This in turn promotes the ability to contribute and build confidence to challenge. Enabling a culture where all four stages can occur will support healthy conflict. During the challenger stage, there is the opportunity for creativity and innovative ideas to surface.

**LEVEL OF
HEALTHY-
CONFLICT**

CHALLENGING
*(CONFIDENT TO SPEAK UP LEADING TO
INNOVATION AND CHANGE)*

CONTRIBUTING
(VALUED FOR CONTRIBUTION AND IDEAS)

LEARNING
(COMFORTABLE MAKING MISTAKES WITHOUT JUDGEMENT)

INCLUSION
(FEELING ACCEPTED AND RESPECTED)

SAFETY LEVEL

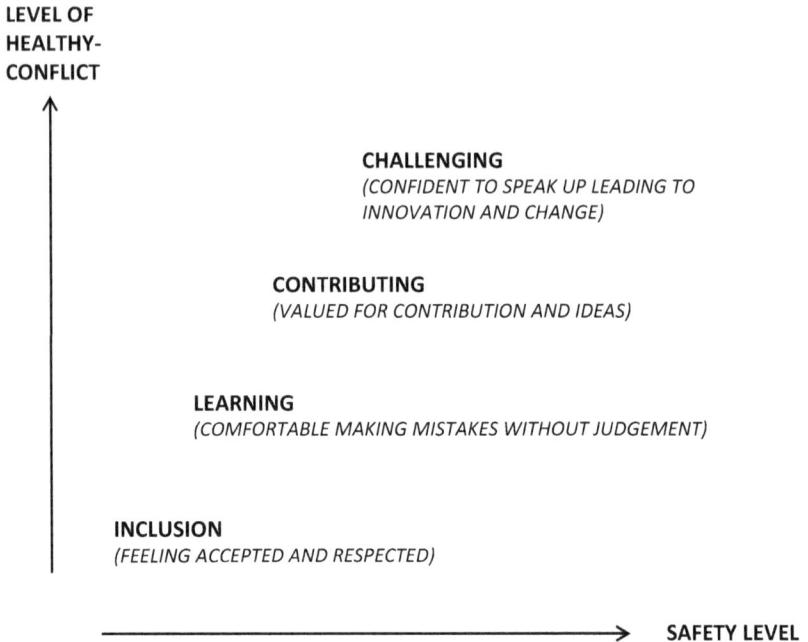

Figure 6.2 How healthy conflict can be achieved with psychological safety, based on *Four Stages of Psychological Safety*, Clark, TR (2020)

Work around or adapt within the culture

Different industries, professions or occupations have varying cultural norms when it comes to conflict which reflects the mixture of communication styles, hierarchy, working styles, contextual situations, and professional values and behaviours. This can shape how conflict is handled within these organisations. For example, there are professions with a lower tolerance to risk such as healthcare where patient safety is paramount, as highlighted by Weaver et al. (2013).

In the workplace, you may have come across phrases such as:

- 'That's the way it's done here' or 'We've always done it that way'.
- 'Don't rock the boat' or 'just do it'.
- 'If it was me ...' or 'Why can't you just do it my way?'

This can create unresolved conflict when people do not challenge the status quo for fear of reprisal. Toxic conflict can also arise as behaviours from situations where opinions or reasoning are not accepted or discouraged. An illustration of this dynamic can be seen in Elissa's example dealing with what she deemed as impossible stretch targets.

CASE STUDY J

Elissa and challenging stretch targets

Elissa was told to find £5 million within the next quarter to fill an urgent income gap as the organisation was off track on their targets. This was the fifth time this happened since she'd been there for two years. She encountered resistance when she attempted to push back to her line manager to advocate a more realistic stretch target, due to his autocratic leadership approach, which was the norm in the organisation. Elissa had a naturally supportive approach and was mindful about protecting her team's wellbeing which was already impacted by previous unexpected target uplifts. She identified and worked through these alternative approaches during coaching.

1. Utilising data such as commercial analysis, customer insight, etc., to influence the leadership to support a lower target.
2. Seeking to understand the rationale behind the target to help her frame this with her team.
3. Building alliances with other departments to garner support for her team in achieving the targets.
4. Proposing alternative solutions such as a phased target with extended timelines.

Elissa adapted her approach to foster open dialogue and constructive feedback with the leadership to protect the wellbeing of her team. Although a lower target was not agreed to, the leadership accepted a phased target. As her team collaborated with other departments, this decreased the pressure on her team as the challenge was shared as they focused on achieving the target together. It also resulted in more ideas to surface as there was a mix of different skill sets and experience from different teams, thus increasing innovation.

Manage interpersonal group stakeholder relationships

Here, group stakeholder relationships are considered as collective groups of individuals rather than isolated individuals. Within organisations, there are different departments or business units, levels of seniority such as job levels, front or back office, unions or employee associations, shareholders, or owners, etc. Externally, stakeholder groups may extend to customers, competitors, suppliers, investors or shareholders, creditors, regulatory bodies, the media, industry bodies, communities, or partners and alliances. Each of these groups may have diverging interests or ideas, power dynamics, rivalries, expectations, or resource constraints. Misalignment of ethics or values can also result in a lack of trust between groups or perhaps external pressures due to uncertain market environments.

Navigating these diverse perspectives makes it challenging when dealing with conflict. The approaches shared in previous chapters can help with managing stakeholder groups, particularly the following from Chapter 2:

- **The TKI framework (Thomas and Kilmann, 1974)** which proposes these five ways of handling conflict: avoiding (you lose, they lose); accommodating (you lose, they win); compromising (you both lose and win); competing (you win, they lose); or collaborating (you both win). For example, if there is conflict with investors or shareholders not agreeing with the strategic directions, it might be useful to adopt a compromising or collaborating mode to get to an outcome that suits all. However, if there is clear data or insight about why the strategic direction should be taken, then competing at some points might be beneficial as the insight is used as evidence to stress the importance.
- **The Power–Interest Matrix (Mendelow, 1991)** provides four approaches for managing stakeholders through: monitoring (minimal effort for those with a low level of interest and power); keeping informed (keeping them updated for those with a high level of interest and low level of power); keeping satisfied (meet their needs for those with a low level of interest and high level of power); or managing closely (key players for those with a high level of interest and power). For example, when managing the media, industry bodies or

customer groups, the situation or timeline can determine how you choose to manage them. Groups can quickly move from being monitored, to managing closely, such as when the industry body produces new guidelines, or when the media takes a particular interest in your industry or the type of work you're involved with.

When to do something different

Whilst some may tolerate situations that do not align with their values, such as working in an organisation that prioritises commercial results over customer satisfaction, when they themselves are not financially driven, others can find this more challenging. For mental health and wellbeing, understanding personal boundaries, evaluating them and determining what to do if they are compromised or violated due to conflict is essential. In Elissa's case, during subsequent coaching sessions, she considered how to safeguard her own wellbeing by establishing necessary boundaries. Recognising the misalignment of her personal values with the organisation, she reassessed her position and place in the business. She took the decision to leave and found an organisation more congruent with her principles.

Thus, there may come a point when self-management of conflict reaches a limit, particularly when repeated attempts or different approaches are tried. This may result in further impact on work performance or productivity for individuals, teams or the organisation. In addition to what you can try yourself, Part 3 explores when it might be beneficial to look to other support to manage workplace conflict. This includes working with professionals who are experts in supporting workplace conflict such as coaches, mentors, or mediators.

Summary

The systemic drivers that occur within an organisational context can be driven by the culture of the type of leadership within that organisation. When you find yourself in situations where yours or individuals you work with have values, beliefs or work styles that are at odds with the organisation, it can be helpful to explore why this might be so a suitable approach can be adopted to manage this.

Key takeaways

- Conflict can arise at any stage of an organisation's lifecycle and can be driven by organisational behaviour.
- Organisational conflict extends beyond individual interactions and may be influenced by broader dynamics such as the organisation's vision, goals, priorities, values, ways of working, resource constraints, etc.
- Individuals may find a disconnect between their values or working styles from the organisations they work in, and choices can be made to try to influence or work around the culture may help.
- There might be times when individuals may need to reassess their position such as when they do not feel aligned with an organisation, such as when repeated attempts to move to healthy conflict have not worked for them.

Reflective exercise

1. Identify at what stage in the organisational lifecycle your organisation is at.
2. What factors have led to conflict you've experienced during this stage of the lifecycle?
3. Which approaches explored in this chapter can you adopt to manage organisation conflict?
4. What is something new you have taken away from this chapter?

References

Barker, J, Tjosvold, D, and Andrews, R I (March 1988). Conflict approaches of effective and ineffective project managers: a field study in a matrix organisation. Journal of Management Studies, Vol 24, No 2, pp. 105–194.

Bennis, WG, and Nanus, B (1986). Leaders: Strategies For Taking Charge. Harper & Row.

Clark, TT (2020). The Four Stages of Psychological Safety. Berrett-Koehler Publishers.

Davis, K (March 1968). Evolving models of organizational behavior. The Academy of Management Journal, Vol 11, No 1, pp. 27–38.

Kilmann, R (2023). Mastering the Thomas–Kilmann Conflict Mode Instrument. Kilmann Diagnostics.

Mendelow, AL (1991). Environmental scanning: The impact of the stakeholder concept. In Proceedings From The Second International Conference On Information Systems, Cambridge, MA.

Meyer, E (2014). *The Culture Map – Decoding How People Think, Lead, and Get Things Done Across Cultures*. Public Affairs.

Mooney, JD, and Reiley, AC (1931). *The Principles of Organization*. Harper & Row Publishers.

Snow, S (2020). Culture add: The antidote to culture fit. *Forbes*. Available at: https://www.forbes.com/sites/shanesnow/2020/06/30/culture-add-the-antidote-to-culture-fit/?sh=7c5ad7911a79 (accessed 8 February 2024).

Thomas, KW, and Kilmann, RH (1974). *Thomas–Kilmann Conflict Mode Instrument (TKI)*. APA PsycTests. Available at: https://doi.org/10.1037/t02326-000 (accessed 8 February 2024).

Weaver, SJ, Lubomksi, LH, Wilson, RF, Pfoh, ER, Martinex, KA, and Dy, SM (2013). *Promoting a culture of safety as a patient safety strategy*. Available at: https://www.ncbi.nlm.nih.gov/pmc/articles/PMC4710092/ (accessed 8 February 2024).

PART 3

7

HOW COACHING CAN HELP

Introduction

This chapter explores how coaching can be used to manage conflict at work. Coaching offers a positive and proactive approach that can be complementary to what you may have already attempted to use when working through any disagreement. We start by covering what a coaching approach is, followed by the types of coaches you might come across in your organisation and others you can engage from outside of your organisation.

Exploring coaching

Coaching is a collaborative approach that supports people to achieve their objectives. Sir John Whitmore's definition of coaching is,

> Coaching is unlocking people's potential to maximize their own performance.
>
> (Whitmore, 2017, pp. 12–13)

DOI: 10.4324/9781041056461-10

He goes on to explain that coaching is more about supporting people to learn, rather than teaching them, which could be seen as telling them what to do. A more facilitative approach which is non-directive focuses on using the coaching communication skills of listening, questioning, and playing back, which are covered later in this chapter. This compares with a more directive approach where you might instruct or advise the other person on what to do. Coaching often includes a combination of both non-directive and directive styles, depending on the coach, the person being coached (coachee), or the situation. A non-directive approach supports the coachee to work through the situation, which can be empowering for the individual. Bob Thomson (2013, pp. 1–4) explains the differences, and this is a useful description I often share with people:

> When you are coaching in a more directive style you are more likely to be looking to solve someone's problem for them or to push them towards a solution that you have in mind. On the other hand, when coaching non-directively your role is to help the other person find their own solutions or to pull ideas from them.

In *The Complete Handbook of Coaching* by Cox, Bachkirova, and Clutterbuck (2010), they introduce coaching as,

> Coaching is a human development process that involves structured, focused interaction and the use of appropriate strategies, tools and techniques to promote desirable and sustainable change for the benefit of the coachee and potentially for other stakeholders.
> (Cox, Bachkirova, and Clutterbuck, 2014, p. 1)

They go on to explain that coaching can be viewed through two lenses.

(1) *Coaching based on theory* which drives the approach used by coaches. Some coaches might choose to specialise in one or more approaches. There are a number of theories relevant to helping deal with conflict which include (and are not limited to these): a person-centred approach developed by Carl Rogers (1940s) that believes individuals have the capacity to fulfil their own potential; psychodynamic approaches that enhance self-awareness and the unconscious that might drive certain behaviours; a Gestalt approach based on Gestalt therapy developed by Fritz

Perls, Laura Perls, and Paul Goodman (1930s), which focuses on aware-ness of patterns of behaviour; or a solution-focused approach which is forward-looking and looks at what the future goal may be and how to achieve it.

(2) *Coaching based on genres and contexts* which are more situational and might be topical in terms of the type of coaching required. In relation to conflict, these could include areas such as (but not limited to): career coaching,which aims to support career-related progress, development, or goals; performance coaching that centres on improving perfor-mance at work; executive coaching or leadership coaching that sup-ports leaders or managers in the workplace to enhance their leadership skills, sometimes specifically focused on particular skills required to aid their professional development; team coaching to enhance how people work together; or cultural coaching to encourage inclusivity, navigating differences or conflicting approaches.

For more information about these and many other approaches, *The Complete Handbook of Coaching* by Cox, Bachkirova, and Clutterbuck (2014) is a great compendium and reference tool.

In practice, both theory- and genre-based coaching are interlinked. Although coaching practitioners may specialise in one approach, many draw on different elements when helpful for their clients or when it's useful for the situation that is being worked through. Some coaches spe-cifically specialise in the topic of conflict resolution to help facilitate com-munication and understanding to find solutions to conflict. Therefore, there may be occasions when you might choose to engage a coach with particular expertise depending on the conflict situation you need support with. Before considering whether to engage a coach to support you, it may be helpful to understand more about the key skills that are the foundations of a coaching approach in case you want to try this yourself or recommend coaching to a colleague or one of your team.

Key coaching skills for helping with conflict

In order to coach effectively, building a relationship with rapport and trust is essential to ensure there is open and honest dialogue. Coaching also has three key fundamental conversational skills which are listening, questioning, and playing back. Each of these is useful when it comes to approaching conflict at work and when used together as a coaching approach, they can help with navigating conflict.

Rapport and trust

Establishing rapport in coaching is essential for fostering trust. Rapport is the connection you have with the other person which can cultivate mutual respect and understanding for each other. This is important for enabling effective collaboration so that both people can have the confidence to have open and honest communication, and this is key to the coaching process. Having both rapport and trust can create a psychologically safe and supportive environment to enable conflict situations to be fully explored and resolved.

Listening

Listening is an essential component of coaching conversations and a foundation for effective coaching. Listening for the purposes of coaching is different from some of the listening that occurs during conversations in our personal or work lives. When coaching, Christian Van Nieuwerburgh discusses listening to encourage thinking, and says,

> For the purposes of coaching, it is important to listen in a way that encourages the coachee to think more deeply and talk more openly.
> (Van Nieuwerburgh, 2017, pp. 27–28)

This type of listening is intentional. Bob Thomson states,

> Listening is an active process – it's much more than sitting passively while the other person talks. It's important to pay attention to both words and non-verbal communication. It requires concentration, and hence it can be tiring.
> (Thomson, 2023, p. 57)

This brings us to active listening which Robin Abrahams and Boris Groysberg explain as having cognitive, emotional, and behavioural aspects:

Cognitive: Paying attention to all the information, both explicit and implicit, that you are receiving from the other person, comprehending, and integrating that information

Emotional: Staying calm and compassionate during the conversation, including managing any emotional reactions (annoyance, boredom) you might experience

Behavioral: Conveying interest and comprehension verbally and nonverbally

(Abrahams and Groysberg, 2021)

Listening is about enabling the other person to share and for those who are listening to comprehend what is being shared. During conflict, active listening can be powerful in itself as the other person is given the space to reflect on what is happening, which can help them understand how to address the situation by coming up with their own ideas. It can also help you focus on the facts and feelings that have occurred, to understand their perspective, and in doing so improve communication to work through the conflict. It's also useful to be aware of other elements of how people communicate to gain an enhanced picture of what the other person is saying such as their:

- Body language refers to the visible actions shown by all parts of the body such as the face, hands, arms, stance, etc.
- Voice which includes the pitch, tone, pace, and volume.
- Words that make up the message being said.

You might have come across Albert Mehrabian's (1967) work which looked at the importance of how a person communicates and his research found that when someone communicates their feelings or attitudes, the way they communicate might be seen as, 7 per cent of the words used, 38 per cent from their vocal tone of voice, and 55 per cent from their facial expressions. It's important to note that these proportions are based on research of when someone is discussing their feelings and does not apply to all communication. However, the concept of communication being more than just the words said can be useful to bear in mind when dealing with conflict when feelings often come into play. This is because conflict can be a particularly emotive situation to be in, therefore considering tone of voice and body language can help in comprehending what is happening when listening to others.

Questioning

The next crucial conversational skill in coaching is the ability to ask questions. Asking questions can help focus or refocus the conversation when tensions run high during conflict. Asking the right type of questions and using an open questioning technique, where there is not a yes or no answer, will enable a deeper level of understanding about what might be driving the conflict. Using words such as who, what, when, why, where, and how can help frame questions that can deepen the dialogue.

It's important to avoid leading questions that encourage a specific answer. This links to how directive or facilitative you might want to be when handling the conflict. For example, if you are adopting a coaching approach, it is not best practice to solve the issue for the other person or tell them what to do (refer to Figure 7.1). A coaching approach would adopt a more facilitative style where you would ask open questions and listen to understand which will enable the other person to work out what they could do themselves.

Sometimes, whilst using a more facilitative approach, the other person may become uncomfortable when they are unable to think of what to do. Rather than jump in with suggestions, adopting an approach that Nancy Kline (1991) encourages of providing a thinking environment, where being able to hold the silence provides the opportunity for the other person to

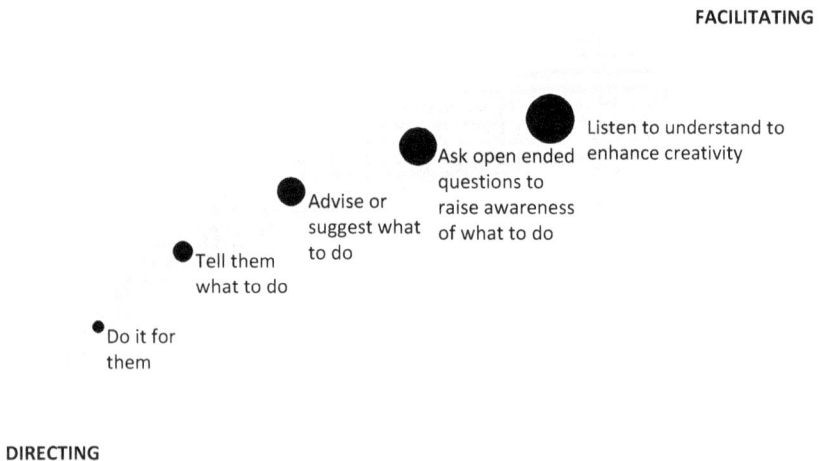

FACILITATING

Listen to understand to
enhance creativity
Ask open ended
questions to
raise awareness
Advise or
suggest what   of what to do
to do
Tell them
what to do

Do it for
them

DIRECTING

Figure 7.1 The directing to facilitating spectrum, adapted from Downey (2003)

think. This can be powerful as they can be persuaded, through the silence, to think more which can help them bring more interesting reflections or ideas to the surface. Asking questions and not providing solutions, enables others to come up with their own way forward that is often better for them and their situation.

Playing back

The third key conversational skill when taking a coaching approach is playing back what you have heard to help you and the other person understand what they have said. This can be in the form of summarising, reflecting back their words or paraphrasing what they have said. Active listening and effective questioning may uncover a myriad of comments, thoughts, and ideas, and it is important that both the coach and coachee fully comprehend this. You might have misunderstood or perhaps the other person has not articulated what they thought and wants to build on it or even changed their mind on what they said. Thomson says, 'The use of summary, paraphrase and reflection give the client the opportunity to look again at their situation ...' (Thomson, 2013, p. 12).

During conflict situations, this voicing out and hearing back what they have said, can bring a different perspective or clarifying perspective to the situation at hand. This provides the opportunity for reflection and reframing of the situation by the client.

This next case study demonstrates how a coach can help an individual move forward with conflict experienced at work.

CASE STUDY K

Fatima and a restructure

Fatima was moved to another role during her department's restructure. She was not happy that her reporting line had changed and her role was now more internally than externally focused. She loved her previous role and team and felt the organisation's decision was not in her best interests. Disheartened, she felt like leaving and arranged for a coaching session with her coach, Ellen, to navigate her next steps.

During their coaching session, Ellen listened attentively to Fatima's concerns and summarised back what she had said, in that the change was uncomfortable and the uncertainty led her to feel anxious about her new role, worried she couldn't cope with the different responsibilities and working with a line manager she didn't know. Hearing this reflection, Fatima immediately gained clarity on her feelings.

Ellen asked questions that encouraged Fatima to explore potential reasons for the restructure. She also provided a safe space and time for Fatima to surface the benefits the new role could bring, such as new skills, diverse responsibilities and expanding her network of stakeholders. As they worked on the next steps, Fatima wanted to explore how she could build a good relationship with her new line manager and came up with some practical actions on how she could do this.

Through the coaching process, Fatima was able to articulate and accept the reasons for the change, recognise the benefits she could gain, and formulate a plan with practical actions for moving forward. Instead of wanting to leave, she was optimistic about the opportunities the new restructure brought to her and felt empowered to embrace the changes with more confidence.

How to use coaching to help with conflict

There are various ways in which coaching can be used to help with managing conflict and there are different approaches that can be useful for you to consider depending on the conflict situation.

When you yourself experience conflict

When you yourself are in a conflict situation and may have tried some of the approaches introduced earlier in this book but are still struggling to make headway, it might be useful to have coaching. An internal coach who is within your organisation may be available to provide this service. Some organisations have a pool of internal coaches specifically trained or qualified in coaching. These could be employees who have a day job within the business and who have developed these additional coaching skills. They may also be coaches whose job is purely focused on providing coaching. Some organisations have a list of these internal coaches and depending on your organisation's policies, you may be able to request their services.

If your organisation does not provide these services, then engaging an external coach from outside could be considered such as an experienced executive or leadership coach. To find a suitable coach, your organisation may have preferred external coaches they work with or a panel where coaches have already been selected and shortlisted. If they don't, you can look for suitable coaches on registers held by professional coaching bodies such as the Association for Coaching, European Mentoring and Coaching Council, or the International Coaching Federation. Considerations that you may also wish to take into account when choosing a coach are whether they are:

- Trained or qualified in coaching so that they have the right skills and knowledge to provide coaching.
- Accredited with a professional coaching body where they will have had to pass certain criteria to gain accreditation.
- A member of a professional coaching body where they will abide by their code of ethics and charters.
- Suitably experienced in coaching, particularly the level of experience you would like or expect them to have.
- Recommended where someone you know has been happy with their service or perhaps testimonials you might see on their LinkedIn profile.
- Have regular coaching supervision to ensure they continuously reflect on and focus on developing their coaching approach. A coach supervisor is different from a line manager, and supervision can be explained as 'a formal process of professional support, which ensures continuing development of the coach and effectiveness of his/her coaching practice …' (Bachkirova, 2008, pp. 16–17). Continuous professional development is key to ensuring they keep developing their knowledge to support their clients.
- Practising responsibly with professional indemnity insurance and complying with Global Data Protection Regulation.

Whether you have the option to work with an internal or external coach, an important consideration is whether you are both able to work effectively together. Coaching is built on rapport and trust, which enables you to have honest and open communication. This is crucial when working through conflict. Coaches often offer a non-obligatory short introductory session or chemistry session where you can both see if you are able to work with each other. If you feel that you are unable to work effectively with a potential coach, it is best to find an alternative coach with whom you are able to work, rather than proceed in the hope that it will be okay.

Some might find it more difficult to build rapport or trust with an internal coach. Internal coaches should be independent and impartial, however, some people can find it hard to be fully open and honest with sharing details of what has happened or feelings they might experience for fear of the potential consequences, particularly if the coach knows the parties involved. A previous client engaged me after having sessions with an internal coach from their HR department. They said they were worried about being too vulnerable and sharing true feelings about how they felt, in case this affected HR's opinion of them and may negatively impact their chances of promotion. We discussed how coaches have an obligation to be non-judgemental and maintain confidentiality. However, my client believed if he shared too much information, particularly about how he felt about the situation, that there was a risk of there being unintended consequences, such as unconscious bias that could impact how they were perceived in the future.

There is also the practical cost element that arises when engaging an external coach. Some organisations might fund this, and where they don't or refuse to you might consider funding it yourself. I have private clients who do this because they find coaching not only helps with the conflict at hand but also provides long-lasting changes that support them into the future, such as developing skills or approaches they can use when conflict arises again and for other workplace situations.

Whether you seek support from an internal or external coach, it can be useful to weigh up the benefits and considerations of doing so in relation to the situation you are in.

When others experience conflict

As a leader, whether you're a line manager, or someone working with others on your team or across the business, there may be times when it might be helpful to adopt the coaching skills covered in this chapter. Using a coaching approach could already be part of the culture of your team or business. In research undertaken by the International Coaching

Table 7.1 Example coaching questions to use when coaching someone to navigate conflict

Exploring and understanding the situation	Tell me about the conflict situation. What could have triggered the conflict? How do you think the other person perceives the situation? What behaviours or actions are contributing to the conflict?
Exploring and identifying emotions	How do you feel about the conflict? What emotions are being triggered by this conflict? Which emotions do you think the other person is feeling? How might these emotions influence the situation?
Identifying values or needs	What values are being triggered for you? … or the other person? What differences are there in your and the other person's needs? What do you really, really want?
Exploring perceptions	How do you perceive what the other person's intentions might be? What misunderstandings might be contributing to the conflict? What assumptions are you making? What might the other person be assuming about you or the conflict?
Identifying options or way forward	What approaches or steps could help to address this conflict? What have you tried so far? What else can you try? Who can help you with this? How can they help you with this? How might you work with the other person to resolve the conflict?
Resolution	What obstacles do you anticipate? How can you overcome any obstacles? What specific actions can you take to work through this conflict constructively? How can you engage the other person in resolving the conflict? What learning have you gained to use for future conflict situations?

Federation and the Human Capital Institute (2019), it was found that what distinguished stronger coaching cultures were those whose managers, leaders, or internal coaches had undertaken accredited training in coaching (2019, p. 13). However, I believe that it's not always necessary to be a trained or accredited coach in order to use the coaching skills of listening, questioning and playing back. By developing and focusing on using those skills, it's possible to adopt a coaching approach in everyday working life. Michael Bungay Stanier discusses how to develop a coaching habit and says, 'Coaching should be a daily, informal act, not an occasional, formal "It's Coaching Time!" event' (Stanier, 2016, p. 7). Honing these skills in everyday work or life can enable them to be drawn on particularly when dealing with conflict, whether it's you engaged in conflict and trying to work navigate this with the other person, or if you are supporting another person to deal with conflict they are experiencing. Figure 7.2 provides some of the types of questions I use when coaching people experiencing conflict that you can draw on when supporting others to work through their disagreements. I also find it valuable to use on myself when I experience conflict.

Conflict coaching

Whilst coaching can be used across any topic, some coaches tailor their approach or enjoy working in specific areas, and clients might prefer to choose someone to work with who has expertise in a particular area. There are practitioners who specialise in conflict coaching where they might use some of the coaching skills covered in this chapter to work with clients specifically on the topic of conflict. Jones and Brinkert (2008) constructed their own model and said, 'Conflict coaching is a process in which a coach and client communicate one-on-one for the purpose of developing the client's conflict-related understanding, interaction strategies, and interaction skills' (2008, pp. 4–5). Their model focuses on providing a way to understand the conflict occurring, plans to manage the conflict and how to communicate in terms of interpersonal behaviours in four stages.

1. Discovering the story which involves uncovering the underlying stories, experiences, or beliefs that may have contributed to the conflict which has resulted in the narrative that is held.

2. Understanding the perspectives of identity, emotion, and power to explore how those involved in the conflict might see each other's or people's perspectives.

3. Crafting the best story which can help reframe the narrative about the situation and to recraft an alternative and more constructive story. This may involve challenging limiting beliefs or exploring how to develop strategies to move forward.

4. Communication skills where developing patterns of interpersonal behaviours may be more effective than actions. This could include focusing on active listening, constructive dialogue, ensuring there is psychological safety or other communication skills that may be helpful to enhance the relationships and help prevent future conflict.

If the whole four-stage approach is followed, it can take time to go through. However, there are elements of the model that can be drawn on when working with people in conflict and I've found using parts of the model useful to focus on with clients in conflict, particularly stages 1 and 2 when we explore what is actually happening during the conflict and how all parties may be experiencing the conflict.

Summary

Using coaching as a positive approach to workplace conflict can complement or build on the other approaches covered in this book. To take a coaching approach, there are key coaching skills you can use so it's not wholly necessary to be fully qualified or accredited in coaching. However, there might be times when engaging a qualified and accredited coach may be useful especially where more expertise or an independent third party is required.

Key takeaways

- Key coaching skills of listening, asking questions and playing back can be used as a positive approach to conflict at work.
- Coaching can be beneficial when you are experiencing conflict yourself, or when supporting others who are in conflict situations.
- Internal and external coaching are options that might also be considered, as they provide impartial and skilled coaching.

Reflective exercise

1. How can you develop the coaching conversation skills (listening, questioning and playing back) to support your team or others when working through conflict?
2. Think of a time when you could have or can use coaching skills with others to help them navigate conflict situations. Identify how you could have or how you can use coaching to support them.
3. What policies or approaches does your organisation have in relation to engaging an internal or external coach?
4. What other key takeaways do you have from this chapter?

References

Abrahams, R, and Groysberg, B (2021). How to become a better listener. *Harvard Business Review.* Available at: https://hbr.org/2021/12/how-to-become-a-better-listener (accessed 15 April 2024).

Association for Coaching (nd). Available at: www.associationforcoaching.com.

Bachkirova, T (2008). Coaching supervision: Reflection on changes and challenges. *People and Organisations at Work,* Autumn edition, pp. 16–17. Available at: https://doi.org/10.1007/978-3-030-81938-5_15.

Cox, E, Bachkirova, T, and Clutterbuck, D (2014). *The Complete Handbook of Coaching.* Sage.

Downey, M (2003). *Effective Coaching: Lessons from the Coaches' Coach.* Texere.

Ferris, SR, and Mehrabian, A (1967). Inference of attitudes from nonverbal communication in two channels. *Journal of Consulting Psychology,* Vol 31, No 3, pp. 248–252. Available at: https://doi.org/10.1037/h0024648.

Human Capital Institute and International Coaching Federation (2019). Building strong coaching cultures for the future. Available at: https://coachingfederation.org/blog/now-available-building-strong-coaching-cultures-for-the-future (accessed 19 April 2024).

European Mentoring and Coaching Council (nd). Available at: www.emccglobal.org.

International Coaching Federation (nd). Available at: www.coachingfederation.org.

Jones, SJ, and Brinkert, R (2008). *Conflict Coaching – Conflict Management Strategies and Skills for the Individual.* Sage.

Kline, N (1991). *Time to Think – Listening to Ignite the Human Mind.* Octopus Publishing Group Ltd.

Stanier, MB (2016). *The Coaching Habit Say Less, Ask More & Change the Way You Lead Forever.* Box of Crayons Press.

Thomson, B (2023). *Coaching from A to Z and Back Again – 52 ideas, Tools and Models for Great Coaching Conversations.* Critical Publishing.

Thomson, B (2013). *Non-directive Coaching – Attitudes, Approaches and Applications.* Critical Publishing.

Van Nieuwerburgh, C (2017). *An Introduction to Coaching Skills – A Practical Guide.* Sage.

Whitmore, J (2017). *Coaching for Performance, the Principles and Practice of Coaching and Leadership.* Nicolas Brealey Publishing.

8

HOW MENTORS AND SPONSORS CAN HELP

Introduction

There may be times when assistance from others can help you move forward, especially if you've attempted to handle conflict at work on your own with limited success or are struggling to know what to do next. If you have a mentor or a sponsor, they can be particularly useful sources of support during these times. While there is some overlap between what mentors and sponsors can provide, knowing when to seek guidance from each can be useful when considering what to do. Both mentors and sponsors can offer support to help your professional development where a mentor can provide guidance, advice and support and a sponsor can actively advocate for you, or open doors to other opportunities to enhance your professional development. If the need arises, both mentors and sponsors can support in situations such as navigating conflict at work. Mentors can offer guidance, advice, and wisdom to help with situations such as conflict at work. On the other hand, sponsors can support you, influence, or may

DOI: 10.4324/9781041056461-11

even intervene in conflict situations. This chapter explores how working with mentors and sponsors can be used as a positive approach to handling workplace conflict.

How mentoring can help with managing conflict at work

Mentors are individuals with valuable experience, skills, and knowledge who can support those developing in a particular area. Whilst they can often be more senior, what matters is their expertise, not necessarily their job title or position. Bob Thomson (2013) provides a clear definition of mentoring.

> Mentoring is a relationship in which the mentor draws on their experience, expertise and knowledge to support and guide a less experienced person in order to enhance their performance or encourage their development.
>
> (Thomson, 2013, p. 5)

Mentors can play a key role as advisors or role models who demonstrate the behaviours or actions that can make a positive impact at work. An important factor that mentors and mentees (the mentee being the person seeking the help) should have is a high level of trust and respect for each other. This enables them to foster a constructive relationship. Mentoring might be in the form of a formal relationship with regular meetings to work through a mentee's goals. Or it may be on a more informal basis where advice or guidance is sought as and when required. There can be benefits in having more than one mentor, such as those with different expertise to support different goals, and they can be within or outside your organisation, and might even be in a totally different industry.

A mentor can provide a safe space for situations to be explored and because of this, provide psychological safety for sensitive issues such as exploring how to manage workplace conflict. Similar to coaches, they can provide a place for reflecting on the causes of conflict and to challenge you to think creatively about what you can do to approach it.

Mentors can provide the following.

- **Active listening,** through listening attentively within a safe space, where concerns, emotions, and the situation can be reflected on.

- **Perspective and insight,** by offering an objective view on the conflict situation along with support in understanding any different views on what may be happening.
- **Experience,** in the form of when they have experienced similar conflict situations and how they managed them.
- **Knowledge and skills** can be shared to transfer valuable insight and skills to manage conflict.
- **Guidance** on how to approach the conflict, how to manage emotions and other stakeholders.
- **Support,** as you go through the conflict and perhaps try out different ways of managing it.

The following case studies present workplace scenarios of how mentoring can help manage conflict at work.

CASE STUDY L

Kim and an international project team

Kim was leading a cross-functional project with representatives from different countries and found they often encountered conflict with some of the project team. Kim felt out of their depth and brought this to their mentor, Zara. After discussing the situation, Zara found that when it came to communication, Kim's approach did not take into consideration the cultural differences which led to misunderstandings. She had extensive experience working with international teams and supported Kim to understand cultural sensitivities and differences, and shared techniques they could use in different situations.

CASE STUDY M

Niko as a new Non-Executive Director

Niko was a newly appointed Non-Executive Director with a start-up company and found when he suggested strategic changes, it led to conflict with the board who saw his suggestions as criticisms that were not aligned to their organisation's culture. He was thinking of resigning from his position and talked it through with his mentor, Cole.

Cole was a seasoned Non-Executive Director in a range of organisations and also had extensive experience as an Executive Director. She helped Niko understand the stakeholder dynamics, how to adapt his communication approach to tailor and build relationships with board members to build trust, and ways in which he could align her suggestions to the company's vision and objectives. This enabled Niko to see this position as a learning opportunity which would enable him to develop his stakeholder management approach, rather than a challenge he was going to walk away from.

How sponsors can help with managing conflict at work

Sponsors are people who are more senior than you and are those who have a vested interest in you and your career development. They can advocate for you at work and can go further in proactively supporting you, as Kate Chambers (2023) mentioned in a LinkedIn article.

A sponsor is someone who advocates for you and your work, who can provide guidance and support, and who can leverage their position of power to open doors and create opportunities for you.

(Chambers, 2023)

Not only are sponsors important for your career, but they can also be instrumental in supporting you when it comes to navigating conflict. Sponsors have a vested interest in how successful you are, so if required there is the option for them to help you look at the conflict and due to their network, which may be at a higher level, help pave the way by influencing at a higher level. In addition to the points highlighted in the previous section on how mentors can help, sponsors can do the following.

- **Influence**, by using their position or authority to ensure conflicts are addressed fairly. At times, their involvement can add weight to achieving a resolution and encourage all involved to engage and constructively work things through;
- **Navigate the internal politics**, as they can provide advice on how to handle disagreements, insight into the unspoken rules that may govern how certain individuals work, and might even get involved to help resolve conflict;

- **Provide resources** in the form of allocating support, whether it's access to funding, colleague support, or other things that may help with the conflict situation. They might also provide additional support to help with professional development in the form of building skills, knowledge or experience. They may also leverage their own network to open doors which could help navigate the conflict.

The following case studies of workplace scenarios demonstrate how sponsors have helped individuals manage or resolve conflict at work.

CASE STUDY N

Resistance to Al's new policy

Al, a mid-level manager, had an idea to implement a new hot-desking policy which would save significant costs on rental space. Early feedback indicated there was already resistance from many people including senior executives who wanted to keep their own desks. Al understood their opinions, but with such strong opposition at this early stage, he turned to his sponsor, Sera, for guidance.

Sera provided strategic advice on how to communicate the project's benefits more effectively, and together they worked through a communications plan. She supported Al by being at the kick-off meeting with colleagues to visibly show her support for the initiative. This gave more credibility to the initiative, and provided Al with confidence and support in how to influence his stakeholders to navigate the resistance to his idea.

CASE STUDY O

Stanley's project concerns

Stanley had been allocated Layla, a project manager, to manage the optimisation of an existing service in line with new legislation. Stanley thought Layla was blasé in the way she managed timelines and the quality of the various activities. They often had disagreements, with Stanley requesting more transparency on the project's progression, and Layla pushing back as she felt he should trust her. Stanley was stressed as their working relationship was strained and he worried the project would not land on time. This came up during a chat with his sponsor, Jin, who happened to be an executive on the Change Board.

Jin spoke to Gal, the Programme Director responsible for the project managers, to understand how his project managers kept their project leads updated. He admitted that it was informal and up to the project managers and project leads to agree on an appropriate process that worked for them. Jin proposed the need for a robust and consistent update process implemented across all projects, and suggested Stanley and Layla lead this for both the project leads and project managers, respectively. This resulted in them having the opportunity to gain best practice from across the business, and indirectly encouraged them to collaborate on a broader issue than their own, resulting in a generic working solution to their disagreement.

Concerns and misconceptions about mentoring and sponsors

You can expect working with mentors and sponsors to be a collaborative and dynamic process, where you both are committed to working through issues in a constructive way. When seeking guidance on managing conflict from a mentor or sponsor, there are some key areas to be aware of.

Empowerment. To avoid dependency and over-reliance, it's key to take responsibility for the situation, and not leave the conflict situation's resolution to mentors and sponsors. There should not be the expectation that they can solve all conflicts. Their role is to support you in navigating how to approach them.

Bias or subjectivity. Be aware of the risk that a mentor or sponsor may have particular views and these can be similar or different to yours. They may not validate your perspective and should provide honest feedback on what they see, which might involve them challenging your own viewpoint or the assumptions you have made. Their role should be to remain unbiased and objective, not take sides and to advocate a positive work environment using fair and constructive approaches. In doing so this can lead to increased insight and perhaps constructive criticism that can help in understanding the issues and how to approach them.

Summary

Mentors and sponsors can play pivotal roles in supporting the approaches you might use to address workplace conflict. How and when you choose to seek support from them will depend on the conflict situation. They can be considered as complementary approaches that can be used alongside the approaches covered in the earlier chapters of this book, rather than used in isolation.

Key takeaways

- Mentors provide guidance, empathy and development support to deal with conflict.
- Sponsors can leverage their influence and networks to influence a fair resolution of conflict.
- The collaborative nature of seeking support from mentors and sponsors can support in developing long-lasting and more constructive or stronger approaches when dealing with conflict at work.

Reflective exercise

1. If you don't have a mentor or a sponsor, think of two or three people who could be potential mentors or sponsors.
2. Reflect on how these mentors or sponsors could support you with navigating the conflict you might have.
3. What is something new you have taken away from this chapter?

References

Chambers, K (2023). Why is having a sponsor at work so important for your career. *LinkedIn*. Available at: https://www.linkedin.com/pulse/why-having-sponsor-work-so-important-your-career-kate-chambers/ (accessed 29 February 2024).

Thomson, B (2013). *Non-Directive Coaching – Attitudes, Approaches and Applications*. Critical Publishing.

9

HOW MEDIATION CAN HELP

Introduction

Mediation is an independent and confidential process that can be a useful approach in helping resolve conflicts or disputes. Mediation comes in different forms and it's commonly used to resolve civil, family, or commercial disputes, and for conflict that occurs within the workplace, there is a specialised form called workplace mediation. This chapter focuses on workplace mediation, what should be considered when choosing to use it, and how it can be a positive approach to addressing conflict at work.

What is workplace mediation?

Workplace mediation is an intervention that takes place in a workplace setting. A third party assists two or more colleagues involved in disagreement to negotiate mutually acceptable resolutions to their situation. The conflict or disagreement is often referred to as a dispute. The Chartered Institute of

DOI: 10.4324/9781041056461-12

Personnel and Development (CIPD) describes mediation as follows on its website:

> Mediation is a tool to resolve workplace conflict or disputes. It's often described as a form of informal or 'alternative' dispute resolution (ADR), as it's less formal than the more traditional grievance and discipline procedures and employment tribunals. It nonetheless follows a structured approach.
>
> Mediation can be used at any stage of a disagreement or dispute. The process is flexible and voluntary, and any agreement is morally rather than legally binding.
>
> (Chartered Institute of Personnel and
> Development, nd)

In the majority of cases, workplace mediation is used when two parties are in dispute, but it is also suitable when more are involved such as teams or groups of people; for example, a line manager and their team.

Principles of workplace mediation

Before considering the use of workplace mediation, there are some key principles that are the foundations required in order for successful mediation to take place. These are covered by Doherty and Guyler (2008, pp. 11–17), where they state that mediation should be:

- *Voluntary*: all parties involved need to agree to the process and want to work through the situation with a focus on and attempt to resolve the dispute. Therefore, forcing someone to undertake mediation should not occur as this might result in a lack of ownership or unwillingness to work through the issues.
- *Solution or agreement-focused*: all parties work together to agree on the way forward. Referring to the Thomas–Kilmann Conflict Mode Instrument (TKI model) introduced in Chapter 2, this might allude to a compromising (all lose and win to some extent) or collaborative (all win) approach to resolving the dispute. There might even be some accommodating (one loses and one wins) involved particularly where there are areas or elements of the dispute where one party agrees for it to occur.

- *Facilitated by an impartial mediator*: so there is fairness and mutual benefit for all parties involved when discussing and coming up with solutions to handle and resolve the dispute. The mediator should not have a vested interest in a particular outcome or take sides on who is right or wrong.
- *Confidential*: to provide psychological safety for all parties to discuss the dispute honestly. This excludes any safeguarding issues, such as where something illegal arises or when someone is at risk of serious harm. Thus, whoever sponsored or instructed the mediation, will not be privy to any of the details discussed or agreed to during the mediation process, unless all parties agree to the disclosure. If mediation is unsuccessful, the mediator is under no obligation to let the sponsor know about this or the reasons for it. If at any point the mediator feels mediation should not progress, such as when a party is not willing to resolve the dispute, then the mediator can simply inform the sponsor that they will not go ahead with the mediation.

Workplace mediation process

Workplace mediation is a process that is not legally binding in the UK (at the time of print), but mediators often include some form of contract or documentation, which may include terms of engagement before mediation starts, and agreement to actions that are agreed to at the end of mediation. If it is conducted in person, it is best practice for it to be held in a neutral location which helps protect confidentiality, particularly if those involved do not want others to know about the mediation. It also enables parties to work through the process somewhere independent and away from their usual place of work. Mediations conducted virtually can provide the required neutrality some parties may prefer, particularly if one or more of them may feel uncomfortable being in the same room as the other.

Workplace mediators might conduct their mediations slightly differently with their own approaches, but generally, the workplace mediation process follows a process similar to that demonstrated in Figure 9.1 and explained in more detail here.

1. **Engagement.** The sponsor engages the workplace mediator – to explain the case as they see it, to understand the mediation process they follow, and to agree costs and timings. The mediator will ensure the sponsor

understands the process, including the need for willingness to participate from all parties involved in the dispute and the confidentiality aspect where anything discussed or agreed will not be shared unless all parties consent.

2. **Agreement to participate.** Before continuing, the sponsor will ensure all parties involved in the dispute understand the process and are willing to participate. The mediator will also make the decision of whether the case is suitable for mediation and agree to facilitate the process if it is. If the mediator deems the case unsuitable for mediation, they will not agree to proceed. For example, this might be if a formal grievance is more suited. The mediator might provide terms of engagement document at this point for all parties to agree to.

3. **Separate sessions with each party.** When there are two individuals involved, the mediator will hold separate sessions with them, usually lasting between one to two hours. With teams or groups, separate sessions will be held with each, for example, if a line manager and their team is in dispute, one session will be held with the line manager and another with the team as a whole or a representative or representatives of the team. During each session, the mediator will explain the process to ensure the party understands it and is willing to continue to take part. They will listen to them share their perspective of the situation, identify issues, explore solutions, and then agree what can be shared in the session with all parties together. Confidentiality plays a key part here because the mediator will only share information in the session with all parties, where consent is provided.

4. **A session with all parties together.** Usually this session can take between one to four hours and is where the mediator sets the tone and explains the process for this meeting, including the ground rules and where each party shares their perspective without interruption. The mediator helps parties identify and agree on the key issues, and then encourages them to explore solutions through brainstorming and negotiating possible solutions. If there are any actions or information all parties want shared with the sponsor, this will be agreed to at the end of this session.

5. **Agreement to actions.** The mediator will document the agreed actions, and include this into a mutually acceptable agreement that all parties will sign or commit to. For actions or information all parties want to be shared with the sponsor, either the parties or the mediator will share this.

Pre-mediation	During-mediation			Post-mediation
1. Engagement 2. Agreement to participate	3. Separate sessions with each party	4. Session with all parties together	5. Agreement to actions	6. Actions undertaken 7. Post-mediation check-in....

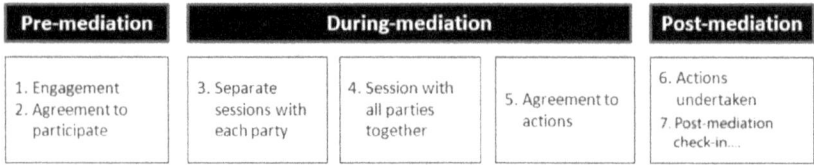

Figure 9.1 Workplace mediation process

6. **Actions undertaken.** After the mediation, the parties will have the opportunity to undertake the actions they have committed to.

7. **Post-mediation check-in.** Some mediators offer a check-in at a certain date following the mediation to see how things have progressed. This is an opportunity for the sponsor and parties to reflect on progress. This could be done via an email or another session which may or may not involve the sponsor.

The mediation (during-mediation in Figure 9.1) can be completed and take place on one day, where the separate sessions with each party take place during the morning, and the session with all parties (joint session) takes place in the afternoon which can ensure momentum continues for both parties. Some mediators may conduct these sessions over more than one day which gives each party time to reflect on what they share and to clarify what they are seeking in a solution. There might be times in more complex situations where parts of the mediation process take longer. These sessions can take place in person or virtually and there are benefits and considerations to think about depending on the case. For example, if one party is worried about physically being in the same room as the other person, then undertaking it virtually may help put them more at ease and they might feel more comfortable speaking honestly and freely.

The mediator or any of the parties can stop the mediation process at any time, and this could be when any one of the parties changes their mind and does not want to continue with the process, when one party's behaviour is unacceptable or if one party might become too distressed to progress.

Workplace mediators

To facilitate mediation conversations, there are various skills a person undertaking the mediation should have. These include key skills of rapport and trust-building; listening; questioning; and playing back. You may recognise these skills are similar to those of a coach as covered in Chapter 7. However, mediation can be more challenging and complex than coaching, because mediators are required to work with more than one party. Therefore, in addition to coaching skills, impartiality is a key component required to be able to conduct a fair and unbiased process for all parties involved in the dispute because they must be able to trust that the process will enable them to work through the disagreement fairly. Similar to a coach, unconditional positive regard for others is key, as is being non-judgemental to parties involved in the dispute, regardless of who might seem to be in the right or wrong. A mediator must not take any sides and remain impartial.

Facilitation skills are a key skill required because a structured process needs to be followed to guide parties through the stages and to ensure they remain focused on resolving the dispute. Encouraging participation from all parties will enable them to express their views and feel heard, which can support some trust-building between them. There might be the need to manage the dynamics between parties, particularly when one is more senior, or when strong emotions or negative behaviours arise that may impact how productive communication is. Thus being able to manage these occurrences can prevent or limit any tensions from arising.

Particular experience with problem-solving or conflict management can also be beneficial in understanding the types of conflict that may occur and how it impacts the parties involved. This can enable them to proactively manage tensions or emotions that may arise during the mediation process. Being able to facilitate the discussions effectively is important to remain focused and hopefully complete the mediation process during the agreed timescales. Most importantly, the mediator needs to be able to structure and manage the conversation. The next case study provides an example of how mediation can help.

CASE STUDY P

Nathaniel and Rosa

Nathaniel, who had been identified as a potential talent in his organisation, was often in conflict with his line manager, Rosa. He felt she favoured other team members by giving them the challenging tasks he wanted. Despite requesting more demanding work to lead, Rosa wanted Nathaniel to focus on supporting the others in the team, as he was already performing well. She thought he was overly ambitious, lacked team working skills, and saw his reluctance to support colleagues as a problem. Their ongoing disagreements were affecting team morale and prompted them to escalate the issue to HR, who recommended working with Mo, an external workplace mediator.

Mo met with each individually and provided a neutral, safe space for each to talk about their perspective on what was happening. This enabled him to gain insight into both of their emotions and the issues that were underlying their conflict. It also helped him to build a degree of rapport and trust with each of them. In the joint session, Mo facilitated open dialogue, helping Nathaniel and Rosa understand each other's viewpoints. In doing so, Nathaniel realised that Rosa aimed to develop his leadership skills through developing and supporting others in the team; and Rosa recognised Nathaniel's desire was for growth rather than her initial belief that he was overly ambitious. This resulted in her agreeing to provide him with more challenging tasks aligned with his development goals. They also agreed to have regular check-ins together to review workload and explore new opportunities for Nathaniel to take on more complex projects while still supporting other team members with their development. Mediation supported them both to identify and address their issues constructively, and find a mutually beneficial way forward that both were committed to.

Internal versus external workplace mediators

It is important to consider who undertakes the mediation, and selecting the right person is crucial to ensure impartiality and to be able to facilitate a fair and structured approach. The person involved in mediating might sometimes be another person on the team, a line manager or someone from outside of the team. Although there may be good intentions, if that person is not fully impartial to the situation it could compromise the process as unconscious bias may occur or parties may lack trust in the process. With untrained workplace mediators, there is a risk the dispute may not be resolved or even escalate further. Mediation when facilitated by an impartial and trained mediator can be more effective in helping those involved in the dispute to reach agreement. Here are some examples of types of people who might be used.

- **Internal untrained mediators.** These can be employees within the organisation, sometimes a line manager may feel they are appropriate to work with their team members to resolve the conflict, or at times a member of the HR team might undertake it. There are advantages in that they are familiar with company culture, it does not lead to additional costs apart from the time invested, and it can be a relatively informal approach to mediation as someone internal facilitates the process, as opposed to the formalities of hiring an external person. However, the approach may lack an effective or structured process and there is the potential for bias to occur, particularly if the employee undertaking the mediation has a vested interest or conflict of interest. There is also the consideration of confidentiality as some of the parties might not feel able to be open and honest for fear of repercussions.

- **Internal trained workplace mediators.** Some organisations might have trained mediators who work within the organisation who have the relevant skills, knowledge and experience to undertake mediation. They will be familiar with the company culture and this can be a cost-effective approach as they are already part of the organisation. As they will have been trained in mediation, they will facilitate sessions using a structured approach that is effective for mediation. However, there are also considerations such as the risk of bias and how confidential the intervention may be because the mediator is part of the organisation where the parties are experiencing the dispute. Conflict of interest and the level of trust might also need to be considered, especially if the internal mediator is in any way connected to any of the parties, such as within their department, works indirectly or directly with them, etc.

- **External trained workplace mediators.** Professionally trained mediators from outside the organisation with the skills, knowledge, and experience to undertake the mediation is another option. A primary consideration is the financial cost involved and whether the organisation is willing to engage in this service. However, despite the initial cost, there are benefits to this approach as they will be impartial, and specialise in the expertise of handling mediation cases, which often results in quicker and more successful outcomes.

When to mediate

Workplace mediation should not be the first thing to consider as soon as conflict arises, and earlier chapters of this book provide approaches to try first. However, workplace mediation can be used early on in conflict situations and *The Gibbons Review* (Gibbons, 2007) on resolving disputes in the UK workplace suggested, 'Early mediation/conciliation in the workplace is the way to resolve disputes before irretrievable breakdown in relations occurs. This is key where people wish to continue working within the same organisation' (2007, p. 33). In the report, recommendation 7 made to the government highlighted that mediation be included as part of the dispute process (2007, p. 39) to reduce the number of cases going to tribunal. This helped raise awareness of workplace mediation as an approach to support managing workplace conflict and it has since been gaining more popularity as a tool to use. When considering the use of mediation, there are a number of factors that might impact whether it is the right intervention to introduce.

It's not a magic wand that fixes everything

In research by the Advisory, Conciliation and Arbitration Service (Saundry and Unwin, 2023), approximately 80 per cent of mediation cases resulted in mutual agreement from those involved in the conflict and a positive outcome. However, there will be times when conflict can remain unresolved or partially resolved. In some circumstances, it may not prevent further conflict resolution steps such as going through the formal complaint or grievance process, or performance management procedures, which is covered in Chapter 10.

May not be suitable for every dispute situation

There are many types of occasions when workplace mediation is particularly effective such as conflict arising from interpersonal conflict, miscommunication, inter-departmental conflict, bullying, harassment, or cultural differences. However, there are occasions when mediation is not the right intervention to use, and this will depend on the dispute case at hand. Some instances when it may not be suitable are when there is severe bullying or harassment, or legal or compliance issues that have been breached.

Another important aspect to consider for when mediation may not be appropriate is where one party may be particularly vulnerable, such as with someone with learning difficulties or someone who requires support with their mental health. More formal approaches are highlighted in the next chapter.

Takes commitment and work from all parties afterwards

The effectiveness of workplace mediation often extends beyond the mediation process. Many misunderstandings can be resolved on the day. However, there will be future actions that have been agreed on during mediation that will need to be implemented post-mediation. Thus, genuine commitment from all parties to follow this through is required, with particular emphasis on being accountable for progress to occur. There may even be the need for further support or resources to be made available to the parties, such as training or coaching to support any agreed actions. All this is key to ensure the situation does not regress back to the conflict or a repeat of patterns of behaviour.

It is an informal process which is not legally binding

An important aspect to consider with workplace mediation is that the process takes place on a without prejudice basis. This means that things discussed during mediation cannot be used as evidence later on in any potential legal proceedings such as an employment tribunal or if the case goes to court. This aligns with the concept of mediation being confidential. Workplace mediation provides a safe space for parties to be open and honest in exploring possible solutions, without the worry that what they say or agree to may be quoted later or used against them. However, it is important to note that there may be occasions when without prejudice does not apply; this could be when all parties agree to waive it and that information is to be shared with others, or when there may be a legal obligation to disclose the information if there is a threat of harm, illegal activity, or if serious misconduct has occurred. Although parties may agree to or sign up to resolve their dispute with actions, there is no recourse that can be taken if they do not follow this through. Workplace mediation is an informal process which often prevents the need for future procedures to take place.

Summary

Workplace mediation is an informal intervention to support the resolution of disputes or to find positive ways forward when there is conflict among employees in organisations. Although it is not a legal requirement, it can prevent the situation from escalating further through to more formal processes such as complaints or grievances and is growing in use in organisations. While it is not suitable for every dispute, it can be highly effective for many situations as it is voluntary and provides a confidential and structured approach for parties to use.

Key takeaways

- Workplace mediation is an informal, voluntary, and confidential process facilitated by an impartial individual who can help resolve disputes while focusing on getting all parties to identify and agree on mutually acceptable solutions.
- The process typically involves stages such as engagement, agreement to participate from all parties, separate sessions with each party, a session with all parties, agreed actions to be worked through, and a follow-up.
- Workplace mediators must be impartial and possess key skills, knowledge and experience and can be internal or external to the organisation.
- Workplace mediation can save time and be a highly successful approach; however, it is not suitable for all disputes and other interventions or processes might need to be considered.

Reflective exercise

1. Reflect on any previous or current workplace conflict situations where workplace mediation could have been useful.
2. Using that situation, evaluate the reasons why it would have been suitable and what the potential outcomes might have been.
3. Explore if your organisation provides workplace mediation and if so, what is the process?
4. What is something new you have taken away from this chapter?

References

Chartered Institute of Personnel and Development website (nd). Available at: https://www.cipd.org/uk/knowledge/factsheets/mediation-factsheet/#:~:text=Our%20 2020%20Managing%20conflict%20in,in%20ten%20use%20external%20mediation (accessed 1 July 2024).

Doherty, N, and Guyler, M (2008). *The Essential Guide to Workplace Mediation & Conflict Resolution*. Kogan Page.

Gibbons, M (2007). *A Review of Employment Dispute Resolution in Great Britain*. DTI.

Saundry, R, and Unwin, P (2023). *Estimating the Costs of Workplace Conflict*. Advisory, Conciliation and Arbitration Service.

10

WHEN MORE FORMAL PROCESSES ARE REQUIRED

Introduction

While the informal approaches covered so far in this book can often help manage workplace conflicts, there might be occasions when they are not suitable or not sufficient, and more formal processes are necessary. This chapter does not cover legal regulations or organisational procedures in any detail. Rather, it focuses on recognising when to escalate to more formal processes, highlighting some types of formal processes that might be available, and signposts to further support.

Recognising when more formal processes might be required

Conflict in the workplace was a key focus area of the CIPD *Good Work Index 2024 Survey Report* (Brinkley, 2024, p. 17–26). It found that a quarter of those surveyed had experienced at least one of the following forms of conflict over the last year (Brinkley, 2024, p. 17).

DOI: 10.4324/9781041056461-13

- Humiliation or being undermined.
- Heated arguments, being shouted at, or verbally abused.
- Sex, race, disability, or age discrimination.
- Intimidation.
- Sexual harassment or assault; or physical threat or assault.

For these types of conflict, seeking support is important to ensure inappropriate behaviour is addressed and to prevent future reoccurrences. Cases such as these might be suitable for mediation if all those involved in the conflict agree that they want to go through that process to support the resolution or a way forward. But there might also be times when it is necessary to invoke a more formal process when mediation is not suitable.

Before pursuing a more formal approach, there are some key considerations that are important to have in mind.

- There is a risk of additional or potential stress and emotional impact involved which could negatively impact your wellbeing.
- The time involved can lead to further delays in resolution or put pressure on personal or work commitments.
- There might be a financial cost in terms of engaging legal support or a potential loss of income if the process includes taking time off work.
- There is the risk that it might negatively impact stakeholder relationships, reputation or future opportunities at work.

Furthermore, there is no guarantee that formal processes will provide a satisfactory outcome and there could be negative repercussions from the parties involved which might exacerbate or complicate the situation further. Even if there is a perceived favourable outcome or a win, there can be considerable toll on individuals. Thus considering these factors can help to evaluate and decide on whether to take a more formal approach.

Navigating formal processes

When the Chartered Institute of Personnel and Development (CIPD) asked respondents how conflicts were resolved, they were allowed to choose more than one response and these were the results:

- almost half (47 per cent) said they let it go;
- 29 per cent discussed it with HR;
- 21 per cent discussed it with family and friends;
- only 17 per cent felt able to discuss it with the other person involved in the conflict; and
- very few took further action with only 5 per cent going to grievance, 4 per cent to mediation and 1 per cent to tribunal.

(Brinkley, 2024, p. 20)

The use of formal approaches can help facilitate addressing conflicts appropriately to promote fairness and transparency. They also ensure compliance with internal organisational processes and the law, such as the Equality Act 2010 that covers direct and indirect discrimination, harassment, and victimisation. Those who have experienced the types of conflict mentioned in this chapter, may not be aware of the types of formal processes that exist or might not be in a position to seek out what is available, especially if their confidence or wellbeing has been negatively impacted by the situation.

Support

When considering taking a formal approach, it is important to prepare for it and seek the relevant support to help navigate what to do. Sources of support might be line managers, HR, union representatives, employee helplines, or legal representatives who can advise on the most suitable process for the situation. If you are a line manager or colleague who observes someone going through any of these types of conflicts, you can play a crucial role by offering emotional support, and practical assistance such as providing witness evidence of the conflict or offering to attend meetings with them. You can also provide information such as company policies, encourage them to report the issue, or escalate on their behalf.

Documenting

Keeping documentation or records of what has been happening during conflict situations can be crucial as written records provide evidence to back up or substantiate what is happening. This will be particularly important if the situation escalates to more formal proceedings. Keeping track of facts by recording times, dates, locations, and specific details of incidents that occur including attempts to resolve or work through the conflict, will create a timeline of events. This helps to identify or show patterns of behaviour that impact the situation, such as in the case of repeated bullying or harassment. It can also support when specific occurrences need verification or if more evidence is required later. An example is when witnesses are required when the time and location details can be useful to find people who were there at the time.

Having well-organised records can support memory recall, particularly when conflict runs over a prolonged period of time. As conflict situations can evoke stress or influence emotions, records can provide clarity and a reliable information source, preventing the risk of having incomplete or inaccurate recollections of events.

Types of formal processes

To take a formal approach, start by exploring the information your organisation has available on its resources, such as the HR intranet, company manual or handbook, or employment contract. If you are a line manager or a colleague not directly involved in conflict, but you witness others involved in it, for example, bullying on your team, you can play a key role in supporting them as a third party. If you are a line manager, you may have undergone training on procedures to follow; if not, it might be useful to seek out this information in case there is a future need to support your team members. Here are some of the common formal approaches that are available.

- **Performance Improvement Plans (PIP)**. PIPs are a structured process to outline specific areas that need improvement with clear goals of what needs to be achieved, such as where changes in behaviour are required.
- **Complaints.** Usually, complaints are submitted in writing to HR, particularly in instances of bullying, harassment, discrimination, or where company policy has not been adhered to. HR will investigate and take appropriate action to resolve it.

- **Grievances.** Grievances are usually raised for more serious occasions, such as unfair treatment at work, or repeated negative behaviours. It enables employees to raise concerns, similar to the complaints process.
- **Arbitration.** This involves a neutral third party, the arbitrator, who reviews evidence to make a decision to resolve conflict. It can be used when mediation has not worked or when a quicker resolution than going to a tribunal or court is required.
- **Disciplinary action.** Disciplinary action can be used to address employee misconduct such as repeated inappropriate behaviour or not complying with organisation policies.
- **Constructive dismissal.** Constructive dismissal is when an employee is forced to leave their job against their will because of the conduct of their employer, such as a breach of their employment contract, gross misconduct, or unfair changes to job duties. The employee might decide to pursue a case against the organisation for constructive dismissal.
- **Tribunals.** Tribunals are specialist judicial bodies outside the traditional court system and provide the opportunity for employees to present their case and receive decisions which are legally binding and can be appealed.
- **Legal action.** Legal action can be pursued via the court system and might be used when other resolution approaches have not worked.

Summary

When in conflict, particularly when more informal approaches have been attempted without success, considering the use of more formal processes can be an alternative option to consider. It is important to seek the appropriate internal or external support, to understand which process is most suitable for the situation, and to consider if the process is worth going through due to the impact it can have on your wellbeing, time, financial cost, personal and work relationships, and career. A key consideration before going to any of the more formal processes is to see if alternative more informal approaches might be more effective, such as mediation covered in the previous chapter, which can be a quicker, cheaper and less stressful approach.

Key takeaways

- It's important to identify when conflict situations might require formal processes. This might be for situations where severe workplace conflict such as discrimination, harassment, or bullying takes place.
- Preparing for formal processes is important and should include documenting incidents, and seeking appropriate support from the line manager, HR, union representation, or legal advisors to advise and guide the process.
- Organisations will provide various resources and guidance on the types of formal processes available and familiarisation of this can be useful to have knowledge of what can be used for more challenging conflict situations that cannot be managed with informal processes.

Reflective exercise

1. Reflect on when you have seen occasions of conflict with other people, where you can support them with knowledge of formal approaches to handling conflict.
2. Identify where you can find information about some of these formal procedures within your organisation, and determine what steps can you take to ensure you are up to date with the formal procedures within your organisation.
3. What is something new you have taken away from this chapter?

References

Advisory, Conciliation and Arbitration Service (nd). Available at: https://www.acas.org.uk (accessed 4 August 2024).

Brinkley, I (2024). *CIPD Good Work Index 2024: Survey Report*. Chartered Institute of Personnel and Development.

Gov.uk (nd). Available at: https://www.gov.uk/dismissal/unfair-and-constructive-dismissal (accessed 8 August 2024).

SUMMARY

As the book draws to a close, let's reflect on what has been explored and discovered. Conflict is an inevitable part of working life and when handled positively it can enable you to have more favourable outcomes for individuals and the work you are involved in. Throughout, this book has delved into various strategies and tools that can be used to manage conflict at work. This does not mean they are limited to your professional lives; you might like to try some of the approaches in your personal lives too.

Part 1 acknowledged that conflict is a normal part of the dynamic environments we work in. We explored useful tools that can be used to help understand and work with conflict to get to healthy conflict and resolutions. Part 2 explored how you can manage conflict yourself. We started by looking at self-awareness, understanding ourselves better to manage conflict within ourselves, before moving on to managing conflict with another person, and how to handle more than one other person such as in a team or the groups you might work in. We then also considered the broader context of the organisational system. Finally, Part 3 covered some alternative approaches to adopt from third-party support, such as coaches, mentors, sponsors, and mediators. These experts bring specialised skills, knowledge, and experience to support you when you might have tried your own approaches without success. We also covered some of the other more formal approaches that might be suitable in various circumstances.

The approaches introduced don't have to be used in isolation and can be combined and adapted depending on the situation. Remember, every conflict situation is different and what has been shared is designed to serve you as a guide. Whether you're dealing with a minor disagreement with a colleague or facing a major organisational challenge, you now have a toolkit of knowledge and strategies to try out.

As you encounter conflict, I hope you'll experiment with the approaches shared in this book. Or use the book as a reference guide that provides you with inspiration to try out some of the concepts. I wish you all the best in navigating the disagreements you encounter and hope that you can harness these situations to get more successful results for you, those you work with and your organisations. I'd love this book to serve you as a guide and a reminder that every conflict situation holds the potential for better outcomes all around. Thank you for taking the time to explore the ideas in this book.

INDEX

Note: Page numbers in **bold** refer to tables.

For Product Safety Concerns and Information please contact our EU
representative GPSR@taylorandfrancis.com
Taylor & Francis Verlag GmbH, Kaufingerstraße 24, 80331 München, Germany